T0381481

Three Towns:
A History of Kitimat

Janice Beck

Edited by:

Kitimat Museum & Archives

James Tirrul-Jones, 1983

Louise Avery, 2009

REPRINTED 1997, 3RD EDITION 2005, 4TH EDITION 2009
KITIMAT MUSEUM & ARCHIVES
ALL RIGHTS RESERVED

Order this book online at www.trafford.com
or email orders@trafford.com

Most Trafford titles are also available at major online book retailers.

Printed in Victoria, BC, Canada.

ISBN: 978-1-4269-2629-7

*Our mission is to efficiently provide the world's finest, most comprehensive book publishing
service, enabling every author to experience success. To find out how to publish your book,
your way, and have it available worldwide, visit us online at www.trafford.com*

Trafford rev. 4/15/10

 www.trafford.com

North America & international
toll-free: 1 888 232 4444 (USA & Canada)
phone: 250 383 6864 ♦ fax: 812 355 4082

Acknowledgements

I owe much gratitude to Gisela Mendel who, ov Mr. and Mrs. H. Evans er the years as Museum Director diligently compiled Kitimat's archives and in so doing has assured a wealth of information about the town's past. I am grateful to James Tirrul-Jones who, as new Director of the Museum, continues such work and initiated this project. Thanks also to the authors whose work appears in the two locally published works: "Time and Place" and "The Voices of Kitimat 1967" who have given an interesting compilation of the general experience in Kitimat.

I also thank Gordon Robinson for his informative and entertaining works concerning Haisla culture. Without his work much of what we know today about the native culture would be lost. Finally, I thank all the present and one-time inhabitants of the Kitimat Valley whose heritage I share.

Janice Beck

Many thanks to the following who donated photographs to the Museum Archives which were used in this history:

School District No. 80

Northern Sentinel Press

Mr. and Mrs. H. Evans

Elizabeth Anderson-Varley

Mrs. Crow

Mrs. Pixie Meldrum

Mr. Charlie Shaw

Mrs. A. Scott C. Graham

P. C. Townsend

Miss Katie O'Neil

Mrs. A. Alexander

Mrs. H. Watkiss

Mrs. G. Drewes

Aluminum Company of Canada

Gisela Mendel

Mrs. C. Green

Mr. R. Green

Nelville Anthony

Mrs. A. Coulton

Kitimat Chamber of Commerce

P. D. Anderson

Mrs. L. Byron

Mrs. N. O'Shea

Mrs. S. Mitchell

P. Jimenez

Mrs. D'Arcy Burk

Contents

Foreword

Even though I'm considered an "oldtime" resident of Kitimat and I've lived firsthand parts of the history presented in this book, **Three Towns: A History of Kitimat**, I still marvel at how rich our history really is. When I came to Kitimat in 1956 everything seemed so new. The smelter and town development had literally been carved out of the wilderness. To a newcomer, the strong impression was that the history of this area began with the coming of Alcan.

As I settled in to the new community, a rich, much older history revealed itself. There were tales from the Haisla people, who had lived here for so many years, and stories of early explorers, trappers, prospectors, homesteaders, adventurers, and, of course, the missionaries. Long before the Terrace-Kitimat rail line was completed in 1955, Kitimat was proposed as the Pacific terminus for the Trans-Continental Railway. Years later, the Grand Trunk Pacific Railroad proposals for this valley set off land speculation in which many fortunes were lost. In many ways the aspirations for growth and development of the first settlers were similar to ours today.

We, in Kitimat, have a unique community and a unique history. While our town was planned and developed from scratch since 1949, our history extends back much further. Janice Beck, the author of this book, is to be commended for her efforts in researching and documenting this history. Anyone reading it will be left with a deeper understanding of Kitimat.

I've often jokingly said that my family came to Kitimat to stay five years and make our fortune. Because we never quite made it, we're still here. Janice Beck even quotes me saying this in her book. The truth is I've stayed because I wanted to. The natural beauty and opportunity present here are found in few other places. In terms of our town and our history, all Kitimatians have good reasons to share the pride I feel for our community.

George Thom (Kitimat Mayor, 1972-1974, 1977-1984)

Introduction

If one was to look no further than the present face that Kitimat presents, it would seem correct to begin this town's history in the early fifties. One would begin with the amazing story of Alcan's (Aluminum Company of Canada) engineering and industrial feat in the northern wilds of British Columbia which saw the construction of the first, "completely new, completely 20th Century town in North America—Kitimat."

Unlike older communities whose growth was dominated by chance and accident, Kitimat is a result of careful urban planning. However, the town, despite its modern appearance, has claim to a history that stretches far back in time, to an era that knew nothing of that space-age metal that has given Kitimat fame as the "Aluminum City".

Kitimat as it exists today owes much to the industrial fervor of the fifties and to Alcan, yet this gives us only a hint of the community's heritage. Beneath the surface and in the memory of those who experienced a different Kitimat lie the clues to this area's historical dawning.

To discover the true beginning of Kitimat means stepping back into that past era and acknowledging the native Haisla culture, the turn-of-the-century missionaries, and a hearty breed of pioneers and fortune-seeking entrepreneurs. The adventuresome spirit and efforts of these people have had as much to do with Kitimat's prominent position on the British Columbian map, as do the events of the past 30 years.

The hopes and dreams of a past generation live on in the present. The pioneering spirit that urged the first explorer to overcome the difficulties of nature, is the same spirit that has, over the years, moved the following generations to make the most of the bountiful coast and valley. Kitimat, as a modern success story, is a logical conclusion to those powerful desires.

Town I
The First Peoples

*Traditional Haisla hammer stone with human face, ladle
with eagle carving, and painted bentwood box piece, all within
the collections at the Kitimat Museum & Archives.*

Chapter 1
Beginnings

Kitimat is situated at the head of the Douglas Channel 70 miles inland from the open water of Hecate Strait and some 500 miles north of Vancouver. It is by any standard isolated. As is the case in many communities which lack the man-made wonders of city lights and skyscrapers, Kitimat is surrounded with the awesome sights of nature.

Flying by jet from the densely populated south to the Terrace/Kitimat Airport is a stunning introduction to the beautiful and, in some ways, inhospitable geography. To European seamen, who first sailed this coast almost 200 years ago, the sea and landscape must have appeared similarly vast and confusing. In this maze of inlets, jutting rock formations, imposing mountains and heavily-timbered landscape, it comes as no surprise that the task of exploring this coastline provided Captain George Vancouver his final and greatest challenge. He and his crew on the ship, "The Discovery", were the first of the early European sailors to sail to the head of the Douglas Channel in June of 1793.

It was a fertile valley that greeted the sailors on "The Discovery". Unfortunately, Captain Vancouver did not think it necessary to record his immediate impressions of the area in his ship's log. The importance of that historical journey, however, did not go unnoticed by the native peoples. In fact, Captain Vancouver and his ship are recalled in the oral history of the Haisla. The tale describes the European sailing ship as a large canoe that at first sight was mistaken for a newly emerged island. The Haisla were amazed to see a ghostlike captain at the helm of the monstrous canoe. This was the first meeting between the two cultures. At the mouth of the Kitimat River, where the present townsite rests, is a flat delta area that was formed over the centuries by the fertile silt left behind as the river was slowed by the sea. The vast delta, now much changed, also marks the site of an old native settlement. This same place provides an

3

entrance into the Kitimat Valley, eight miles wide and almost 40 miles long, ending only when it meets the Skeena River.

The mountain elevations indicated on today's maps are potentially misleading for those unfamiliar with the area. The large coastal range seems impassable on either side of the valley. The rivers and streams are teeming with fish and the woods are abundant with wildlife. The climate, warmed by Japanese currents, is relatively mild and so provides a perfect habitat for dense and highly commercial forests. Cedar is particularly abundant and is of central importance to native technology. It was used extensively for canoes as well as baskets, boxes, rope and art objects primarily because of its resistance to decay, and the ease with which it can be worked.

Despite Captain Vancouver's voyage into the recesses of the Douglas Channel, Kitamaat, the historical and present-day spelling of the Haisla main village on the Douglas Channel, remained a secret, unmarked on the coastal maps of that period. It wasn't until the mid-1800s that surveyors hired by the Hudson's Bay Company included the name on their admiralty charts. Upon this inclusion, change became inevitable. Captain Pender, in the employ of the dominion-wide Hudson's Bay Company, traversed the channel in 1867 and made the first recorded visit to the Haisla village. It was he who introduced the inhabitants to a substantially different kind of economic scheme. The days of relative isolation were over and activities of traditional life branched outwards to become part of a much larger scheme. Commerce was upon them.

People of the Snow

Kitimat has a history which began thousands of years ago. The tales of the Haisla people tell of that time. In these tales, passed by word of mouth through the ages, Kitimat's first inhabitants are recalled. These stories describe a time so distant that it seems only to exist in the mind of the teller. Yet, to be sure, the words hold much truth: heroic deeds, astute explorers and horrific encounters serve as memorials to a past age.

It is told that during the final stages of the ice age, adventurous Indians along the coast were exploring the coastal waters from Bella Coola to Prince Rupert. As was the custom after long winters, groups of men would set out on expeditions. One such group, on a customary spring voyage, ventured up the winding channel and entered the Kitimat Arm. A frightening and unforgettable sight lay before them. In the distance was a huge monster, so large that its gnashing mouth constantly opening and closing could be seen almost 15 miles away. The natives, afraid for their lives, fled the scene hastily. They immediately told the inhabitants of nearby villages of this terror and for years after the Kitimat Arm was deemed unsafe and referred to as "The Place of the

Monster". So it was that Kitimat was left unpopulated for a very long time. Many years passed and still no one dared journey back into the monster's lair.

In a village some distance south of Kitimat Arm, an unfortunate accident occurred that brought the first inhabitants to the Valley. Waamis, better known as Hunclee-qualas, The Archer, fled his village after killing his wife in an accident. Hunclee-qualas sought refuge from his father-in-law at a place where no one would follow. He traveled up the inlet in his canoe, muscles taut and ready for the terrible encounter that lay ahead. In the distance he saw a mass of seagulls feeding on the eulachon that filled the waters. He carried on, for he now knew that the legendary monster of Kitimat was nothing more than this flock of seagulls which from a distance looked like a giant mouth opening and closing.

Hunclee-qualas settled in the Kitimat Valley and found fish, game and berries plentiful. He sent a message of his good fortune to the surrounding tribes and soon many people joined him. Eventually a new tribe known as the Haisla, or "People Who Live at the Mouth of the River", came into existence. The Haisla actually trace their origins to two great nations: The Kwakiutl and the Tshimshians. Their language belongs to the Kwakiutl group.

The name "Kitamaat" was bestowed upon the new Haisla tribe years after they had settled permanently in the area. The new name was first used by a group of Tshimshians, who, during a winter bartering trip, set eyes upon a mass of human heads, seemingly moving without legs along the snow-covered shoreline. "Git-a-maat", said one. There pass "The People of the Snow." It seems that the Haisla men had dug paths through the deep snow and were only partially visible.

Gordon Robinson wrote, "Life in old Kitimat prior to its discovery was entirely satisfying. Satisfying, that is, when viewed through the eyes of the inhabitants of that time. Wants were few, and there was an abundance of materials readily available in season to satisfy the people's needs for housing, clothing, food and an easy means of transport." The comfortable lifestyle offered little reason for change. While the civilizations on other continents were actively engaged in conquest and discovery, the Haisla maintained a means of existence and culture that seemed beyond improvement.

For many years the Haisla lived in the Kitamaat area. Periodically, they would move the permanent village or winter camp to strategic locations to guard against attacks from the Haida people of the Queen Charlotte Islands who were notorious warriors. The permanent village was the base for most of the activities and it was here that the women and children spent a great deal of time. It is believed that the Haisla winter village changed locations several times over the years. Evidence of settlement can be found near the present-day Haisla Bridge, on Minnette Bay, and at the mouth of Anderson Creek. The Haisla eventually settled at Tsimotsa or Snag Beach, site of present-day Kitamaat Village.

"At one with nature"

When white men first made contact with the so-called primitives of the Pacific Coast, they believed that native culture was inferior and unsophisticated. It wasn't until much later, when people began to live among the natives, communicating with them in their own language and sharing their daily activities, that it became clear that the old stereotypes about primitive ways were false. Although the strangers who befriended the Haisla could not help but initiate change with different ways and outlook, many did respect and appreciate the native's inventive and unique lifestyle.

To the newcomers, the Haisla way of life was certainly intriguing. At first, it was evident that the Haisla had a zeal for life as well as a sympathetic relationship with the land they so profitably inhabited. An old Haisla saying typifies that reverential outlook: "Mistreat not the frogs, toads, birds, fishes, nor any small animal for as you treat them so shall you be treated." So it was that the Haisla maintained harmony with nature.

The seasons were a great influence on Haisla activities. The rhythm of nature and that of the natives were perfectly synchronized. The seasonal appearance of the eulachon or candle fish, the midsummer berry harvest, the salmon runs and the inevitable arrival of the biting cold winter kept the villagers busy.

Eulachon harvest on the Kitimat River, 1946

The coming of warmer weather and longer days meant intensified activity for the Haisla. Dried meat, berries, and eulachon oil had depleted over the winter months so it was time again to replenish the supplies.

When the large schools of eulachon arrived in mid-March, the entire village, young and old would be waiting, prepared for the catch. The mood was festive; crowds of people stood on the river shore pleased at the sight of the silver multitude, which filled every inch of the water. Later a feast would be prepared. The fish smoked over open fires would fill the air with a distinctive aroma, fuelling the crowd's appetite and spirit.

The eulachon was a necessary and important resource. Flavoursome when freshly cooked, its excess oil, once extracted and stored, could be used for many months after. The oil was valued by the natives as both a trade item and an important source for vitamins and protein. It was an addition to every meal and even berries were doused in it before eating.

It was the process of extracting the oil that required a concerted effort by everyone in the village. Months previous, the women would have carefully crafted the funnel-shaped nets used to fish the eulachon out of the river, and the men would have prepared the dugouts, boilers and caskets for the heavy labours expected of them during the spring run.

Once the nets were full to bursting, the fish were dumped into the canoes and brought to shore, deposited in large bins, then left to partially decompose in the spring air. To the unaccustomed nose, the smell of the dead fish was quite horrid! One missionary on recording the great "Fish Festival" made the following comment: "The oil or tlatte, as it is called at Kitamaat, has a most dreadful odour, which I cannot even attempt to describe." After sitting for nearly two weeks in the bins, the fish were placed into large, oblong wooden tubs, water was added and the soup was brought to boil by adding red hot stones. After stewing for several hours the rendered oil was skimmed off the top and transferred to boxes, boiled again, strained and finally stored in cedar boxes for future use.

The Haisla depended also on the large numbers of salmon, which were caught each year as they made their way up local streams and rivers. These fish dried well and were ideal for storage.

As the summer months progressed and the days shortened, the Haisla prepared for the annual trip down the channel to spots where salmonberries and huckleberries grew in large quantities. These the women would harvest in cedar bark baskets, the young scrambling at their feet. While the women stayed close to camp and the berry bushes, the men would hike to an area high above to hunt the mountain goat. If the hunt proved successful, the animal would be barbecued around the evening fire and sealed into containers for storage. The goat's wool that had served the animal so well in its cool mountain habitat would come in handy for making warm winter clothing.

"Vital Concerns"

In their efforts to contend with and master their environment, the Haisla can be considered great inventors. Other cultures, possibly more than they realize, inherited from the native people's unique innovations that had grown out of local necessity.

The canoe was important for transportation as well as serving as a symbol of prestige and wealth. The large cedar trees, from which the canoes were fashioned, had to be carefully chosen. It sometimes took up to three days to fall a good, solid tree. This done, the natives used fire to burn the end of the tree and shape the inside of the vessel. This was no easy task.

According to G. Robinson, other people, having heard that the Haisla used fire to build canoes, found a suitable tree, set fire to it, and left. On their return they expected to find that the flames had built the canoe. Of course, only ashes remained. Traditionally, the flames were controlled by using damp sand. The sand was used to trace an outline of the desired canoe onto the log. G. Robinson has said, "If one was skilful enough, he need only remove the charcoal and his canoe would be ready."

One of the most well-used products of the coastal craftsmen was the bentwood box. They were made by kerfing planks of cedar across the grain at points which were to form the box's corners, then steaming the wood until it was pliable enough to bend at right angles. Some of these boxes were often as large as six feet on a side and decorated with relief carvings and paintings.

The winter village of the Haisla provides the best example of efficient housing, as well as the native craftsmen's expertise. In a sheltered area along the shore, large rectangular houses were erected on frameworks of heavy posts and supporting beams. The strong walls were made from heavy cedar planks, many of these several feet wide. The roof was gabled and provided an excellent rain cover. Usually the entrance way and frontal posts were decorated with carvings and/or paint. A whole row of such dwellings facing towards the sea was an admirable sight.

Another vital concern, following transport and shelter, was clothing. The innovative nature of the Haisla and their resourceful use of the natural materials at hand was particularly apparent in their traditional garments. In late spring, the women would climb Yellow Cedar Mountain, a small mountain near the present smelter site. Here they would spend hours stripping the bark from trees. The bark collected in varying widths would be tied into bundles and, later in the day, taken to a particular slough down on the mud flats. Here the bark would be left for up to a month, softening the inner bark. The rough outer bark was discarded and the more pliable material which remained was taken away and beaten with heavy rocks until it was transformed into a full and woolly mass. This fluffy fibrous stuff could be spun and then woven into blankets and cloaks. A finished article made from the bark cloth was softer than wool, warm and weather-proof. It was so strong that it often lasted the span of an owner's lifetime.

"Continuity and Custom"

Although Haisla society was small in scale, its organization and rules were complex and as necessary for survival as hunting and fishing. Unity was of the utmost importance, both in the immediate family and in the clan. The traditional roles and patterns of behaviour had to be accepted by each individual, if the group as a whole was to prove successful.

A Haisla bentwood box acquired by George Anderson in the late 19th Century and later returned to the Haisla people by his daughter, Elizabeth.

The five major clans: Beaver, Raven, Eagle, Blackfish, and Salmon, were a unifying force in the Village. Everyone from slave to nobleman had the comfort and the security of belonging to a clan. The members of each clan worked together in everyday matters. The animal after which each clan was named served as a crest; and those united under a particular crest were the recipients of certain territorial rights and special knowledge that included dances and ancient stories.

The potlatch was an important ceremony for all Pacific Coast natives and the Haisla were no exception. Potlatch, a Chinook word that literally means "to give" was a festive occasion. The potlatch marked major changes in one's life and society. It was also an important part of the economy for the ceremony included giving away goods of great value and an obligation that those who received would be the next to give. The potlatch was greatly criticized by those who did not understand it. The missionary, Thomas Crosby, had this to say about the potlatch: "Of the evils of heathenism, with the exception of witchcraft, the potlatch is the worse, and one of the most difficult to root out." Crosby goes on to describe it as, "The giving away of everything a man possesses to his friends. In return he gets nothing except a little flattery, a reputation for generosity, and poverty."

Potlatches, especially large ones, required considerable preparation. For many months or even years before the event, members of the host's family hunted, fished and worked hard to amass the amount of food and goods required for the ceremony. When the day of the great event arrived, all the property was brought forth and exhibited in heaps within and around the host's lodge. The guests were then arranged according to social position in the tribe, the first or inner row being chiefs. The presiding chief or host would then deliver an introductory speech, recalling the prestige and grand deeds of his ancestors, comparing them with his own exploits and position. The chief's assistants, usually members of his own clan, then called out the names of each recipient, giving the amount and description of the property they were to receive. One would never refuse a gift. Instead it was expected that at a later potlatch, one would give back, with added interest, a similarly worthy gift. In some ways the potlatch and its extensive gift giving can be viewed as a kind of savings bank. One person entrusts another with wealth he possesses, so that at a later and possibly less prosperous time, he will receive the goods and food back with interest.

The Haisla people through experience and adventure developed a culture and a way of life that lives today. They have travelled far, from the great settlement of the Kitimat Valley through times of peace and war to the eventful contact with a fur trader called 'Old Frank'.

Old Frank

Frank Armstrong was the first trader in the area, and finding the Kitimat Valley a tempting place for habitation, settled in to live at the Indian village. He built himself an admirable home in a style drastically different from the ones surrounding. The Haisla were intrigued with the bearded fur trader as well as his solidly built house. The men saw the added benefits of such a weather-proof and completely winterized home, and asked Old Frank to help them build a few of these fine structures.

Armstrong, when not out setting traps or plying his trade, set up his portable sawmill and cut lumber for his native neighbours. From then on, most of the native homes were built following the style of frame construction. The face of the village changed and the cedar beam houses became obsolete. Soon Christianity was to enter the picture, and life considered so perfect, so satisfying, was to be transformed.

Chapter II
Arrival of Christianity

Christian missions played an expanding role in the growing province of British Columbia. From the onset of commercial development around Victoria, it was apparent that the native population suffered difficulties adjusting to the new way of life. Thomas Crosby, a pioneer missionary wrote, "They came under the influences of vile liquids supplied by unscrupulous traders." Large fortunes were made by those who sold liquor to the natives. The traders often took advantage of the native population's unfamiliarity with European culture. The local natives were left powerless, sick, and demoralized.

A Methodist Sunday School was opened in an old barroom in downtown Victoria in hopes that the natives would find help in the Christian gospels. The school was a great success. Crosby wrote of the first missionaries, "Little did those earnest souls think that they were kindling a fire that would spread to have far-reaching results." The Superintendent of Methodist Missions in B.C., Reverend William Pollard, led the meetings at the newly renovated barroom. His teachings attracted a crowd of natives. Among Rev. Pollard's first converts was, Wahuksgumalayou, a man from the Haisla village at Kitamaat.

The Coming of Christianity to Kitamaat

Wahuksgumalayou had travelled by canoe to Victoria in 1874 to trade furs. Instead of returning to Kitamaat as planned, he found a job at one of the local sawmills. There he met a group of Tsimshian who had recently converted to Christianity. They invited their new friend to a Sunday service at the Methodist Hall, in hopes that he too would find the Christian gospel compelling. At that meeting he listened to Rev. William Pollard, who in tender simple words recalled the story of the Creator. The words gave Wahuksgumalayou the "calm of utter peace, implicit trust in God the Father, and hope of immortality." It wasn't long after his initial introduction to the gospel that Wahuksgumalayou was baptized and adopted the Christian name Charlie Amos.

By all accounts, Charlie Amos was an exemplary member of the church. His religious fervour was so marked that Rev. Pollard himself noticed the young Haisla man and decided that he would be a good candidate for further education. Pollard gave Amos the job of ringing the church bell and began to teach his convert how to read and write. For two years Charlie lived in Victoria and continued his involvement in church activities.

In 1876 Charlie Amos returned to Kitamaat carrying with him a bible and a letter stating that he had become a Christian. As Crosby recalls, "Amos was eager to tell the good news to his fellow tribesmen." Several Haisla converted to Christianity. This small group led by Amos held weekly prayer meetings. The elder Haisla were enraged! They saw the new way of life proposed by Amos as a threat to village order. Crosby wrote that, "A bitter struggle between light and darkness began."

Amos and his fellow Christians were excluded from all village activities. The Village Council was further angered by the Christians' disregard of their power. They retaliated by cursing the Christians: "Thus shall you Wahuksgumalayou and your family and friends perish and vanish from the earth. Your names shall not be handed down. You Wahuksgumalayou shall be the last to perish and shall see all your friends pass before you."

The Village elders had good reason to be suspicious of European religion. Other European influences had brought havoc to the Haisla village. Smallpox, once unknown to the natives, had severely depleted the population and alcohol was having its debilitating effects. So it was no wonder that the elders met Charlie Amos' good intentions with anger and disbelief, for they were struggling to maintain their once successful way of life.

The Christians, however, were not easily intimidated. Their strength and sense of purpose charmed Chief Jasee of the Beaver Clan. He encouraged Amos and gave the Christians his undying support. The rift between council members brought more converts and soon there was a group of 70 Christians. It was then that Charlie built the first church in Kitamaat. It was a small log building that served as a schoolhouse and a place for prayer. Gordon Robinson wrote that the little church was "a physical sign that Christianity had overcome heathenism in the Haisla Village."

In 1877 Charlie Amos decided that a teacher was needed to stabilize the Christian community. He travelled to Metlakatla and attempted to persuade Reverend Duncan, who was in permanent residence there, to accept the position in Kitamaat. Duncan, unable to leave his mission for that length of time, directed him to Reverend Crosby at Fort Simpson. He too was unable to leave his mission, so Amos returned to Kitamaat in the first part of the New Year accompanied instead by George Edgar, a native Tsimshian teacher, his wife and two children. They took up residence with Charlie Amos until they could build their own home. Although Christianity was becoming more accepted by the Haisla, Edgar and his family were met with some opposition. Chief Jasee once again came to the Christians' rescue and promised protection for the new teacher. For two years Edgar resided at Kitamaat.

Thomas Crosby of Fort Simpson kept in close contact with the growing Christian community at Kitamaat. He visited the village on numerous occasions and witnessed its transformation. When Edgar left in 1880 it was Crosby who arrived at Kitamaat with a carpenter and a schooner full of lumber to help build a new church. The foundation was laid on the ground where Charlie Amos' log church had stood. A two-room mission house was also built to which Amos later added a cedar slab lean-to.

Charlie Amos as depicted in an early issue of the Na Na Kwa, a Kitamaat Mission newspaper.

For two years following Edgar's departure, there was no permanent teacher at Kitamaat. The Rev. Crosby at Fort Simpson began looking for a teacher or missionary to permanently reside at Kitamaat. In the interim, Amos assumed the position of religious leader and continued to play a crucial role in the conversion of his people. Thomas Crosby remembers Amos as a man who "ever stood faithfully by the missionary." Charlie Amos lived until 1891, long enough to see the gospel extend among his own people and along the coast until many hundreds had professed conversion. His tombstone bears the inscription, "First local preacher of the Methodist Church to the Kitamaat. He giveth his beloved sleep."

Miss Susannah Lawrence

On hearing of the need for a missionary at Kitamaat, Miss Susannah Lawrence volunteered to take the position. She had come west from Ontario to take over the post as teacher at the mission house in Fort Simpson, but when Rev. Crosby described the village at Kitamaat she jumped at the chance.

It was an immense challenge to accept, especially for an inexperienced white woman. The hardships and excitement were highly unusual experiences for a slight and educated Victorian female. In a newsletter called the "Na Na Kwa" or "Dawn on the North Pacific Coast", published by a later missionary, Miss Lawrence recalled her first trip to Kitamaat. "So the last of October, the seven of us started off with Patrick Russ and his wife. Patrick was to act as interpreter. It took us 10 days going a journey of 160 miles, the first day we went 50 miles, stopped at Inverness where there was a large salmon cannery. Came on a terrible storm, rain, hail and snow. About the middle of the night I was called up and found our canoe had been driven under the wharf and filled with water. We had all the provisions for the winter; lumber to build a house, doors and windows also goods for a little store. My trunk was on the wharf tipped on end, the water running out of it, all my books and little treasures were destroyed. It took all the next day to dry our things. The little gentleman at the cannery was determined I should go back and wait for spring, but I could not think of it, feeling God had called me, and those people had been so kind in coming all that way for me. So the next morning we started off again, travelled all that day, in the evening went ashore and pitched our tents. During the night there came a most terrific windstorm, we were obliged to remain for four days. Had pleasant weather the rest of the journey. Arrived at Kitamaat the third of November; it would be impossible to describe the scene on shore when we arrived, nearly all the village came down to meet us with torches as it was very dark. They were all talking together, each one wanted the canoe brought their way, at last after a great deal of trouble we landed. They all escorted us up to our home. They were all so kind I could not help loving them and have ever since."

The first of the many tasks to be completed before Susannah could begin a routine of preaching and teaching was the building of a mission house. The house when complete was to provide living quarters for Miss Lawrence and Patrick Russ and his small family. It was only a two-room affair, but completely

First white woman at Kitamaat: Miss S. Lawrence, picture from the Na Na Kwa

satisfactory in the eyes of the missionary. "I never felt so proud of a home and did not envy the Queen on her throne. Patrick made me a bedtable and a bench out of the lumber we had brought with us."

Life at Kitamaat was busy. Patrick Russ had taught some of the young men to read from bibles but most of the Haisla had little knowledge of English. Susannah Lawrence initiated weekly classes in reading and writing and found that the young women learned very quickly. Every evening there were prayer meetings and on Sundays the entire day was devoted to the gospel. Miss Lawrence had an early meeting at six and then another at half past ten. The one o'clock Sunday service took the form of religious instruction—using brightly coloured pictures of biblical stories. In the evening, Miss Lawrence and her Christian following went out two by two visiting and singing hymns for the sick and elderly in the village. The end of the week was Miss Lawrence's favourite; for every Sunday brought more converts and the fruits of her labours could be plainly seen.

Miss Lawrence's feminine instincts brought a new subject for instruction to the Kitamaat Mission. She took it upon herself to teach the native women in domestic and health science. Using an interpreter she spoke of home cleanliness and nutrition and showed the ladies how to knit and crochet. These duties were to become an essential part of later missionaries' duties. Health education played a crucial role in halting the breakouts of fatal illness as well as preparing the young women for the duties expected of them as wives and mothers.

Patrick Russ eventually left Kitamaat, leaving Susannah on her own, one hundred and sixty miles from any other white person. He had to return when Miss Lawrence's health began to fail in 1884. After two strenuous but successful years as teacher and missionary, Miss Lawrence left the Haisla village. Thomas Crosby credits her with many good deeds. He sums up her two-year stay at Kitamaat in this manner, "It was during Miss Lawrence's time at Kitamaat that the strong hold of heathenism was finally broken up."

It was George Robinson, a lay preacher, who took over from the ailing Miss Lawrence. Robinson had worked in many parts of British Columbia but not always in the capacity of preacher. He was an easterner who had come west for adventure and enterprise. He had lived in Victoria for a time and was employed in Wilson's clothing store. He developed a keen interest in native life and is rumoured to have been the man who gave Charlie Amos his first bible.

After leaving Victoria in 1865 he went to the Queen Charlotte Islands to supervise a local mining venture. It was there that he decided to combine his Christian beliefs and interest in the natives' welfare and enter into full-time missionary work. He taught at Bella Coola, Skidegate and Port Simpson before coming to Kitamaat in the latter part of 1884. George Robinson taught school in Kitamaat for a number of years and eventually married a Kitamaat noblewoman, Kate. George retired from the mission and opened a general store in the village, devoting himself to his family and friends until his death in 1921. The lay preacher and storekeeper left a memorable line of descendants who even today are distinguished personages within the village.

Chapter III
A new phase

In 1893, Reverend George Raley, Kitamaat's first ordained minister arrived. He was sent by the Methodist Church of Canada. Raley was an eager and devoted missionary. The two-room mission house and small church that greeted him seemed inadequately small. As funds became available Raley began concerted work to improve the mission conditions. Raley's years of work at Kitamaat are memorable ones. He began the building of a school for Haisla children. He also published the newsletter called the "Na Na Kwa," led a Temperance Society, opened a weather station, and for 13 years, made Kitamaat his home.

Reverend G. H. Raley, Missionary

The old church at Kitamaat in the winter, ca. 1914

Of his first day Rev. Raley wrote: "On our arrival we found less than a dozen people at home and the village was overgrown with weeds. Indians began to return from the canneries but it was October before the village had its usual number." Rev. Raley had arrived at the height of the fishing season.

It was no longer the custom for men to leave the village to fish for winter stock. Instead they hired on with the canneries at Rivers Inlet, who paid cash for fish and labour inside the canning plant. This new form of employment ushered in a new way of life for the Haisla and new concerns for the missionary at Kitamaat.

Fishing for Cash—Rivers Inlet

In 1867 the salmon canning industry had begun on the Fraser River. From the south it eventually spread into the north coastal areas. During the operation of the canneries at Rivers Inlet an interesting pattern of existence developed for the Haisla.

In 1882 two entrepreneurs, Robert Draney and Thomas Shadbolt had brought Rivers Inlet's first cannery into existence. Although canning was a by-product of new industrial processes, the salmon canneries at Rivers Inlet still relied heavily on manpower. The salmon were caught by hand, cleaned, sliced by hand, and packed by hand into cans.

Cannery at Rivers Inlet, Courtesy of the Vancouver Public Library

One report published in the Na Na Kwa newsletter describes the process: "We step inside the splitting room and see the fish knee deep on the floor as they are thrown from the elevator which brings them up from the scow. Next we see the men at the benches splitting the fish and cutting the fins and heads and tails off. The fish are then passed into the tub where the Indian women armed with knives and scrubbing brushes remove every scale and bit of slime, then we see the fish put on a cutting rock which revolves and cuts them into desired size for the filling process—which is done by more native women. Thence the cans are taken direct to the wiping machine along the endless belt to the soldering machine. From here the cans are hauled to the testing chamber thence to the retort, where the fish is cooked. Next the labels are rolled on and the cases made and filled with cans."

It was not difficult for the Haisla to find employment in the fishing industry. The isolation of the canneries and the small population of settlers left the Indians as the only available labourers.

The traditional methods for salmon fishing—spears, traps and nets—were outlawed in 1892. So it was that fishing offshore from canoes and skiffs became the most popular method. The cannery owners were in such need of native labour that they would send tugboats to Kitamaat every June to tow a train of canoes to Rivers Inlet. They would return the canoes and men in early September when the season had ended. The men received a price for every pound of fish caught. Their wives spent the entire summer inside the factory. The canneries provided quarters for the workers and stores for them to buy necessary supplies.

For many years the Haisla natives made the trek to Rivers Inlet. John Pritchard, a scholar knowledgeable of the turn-of-the-century Haisla predicament has written: "It is safe to say that from around the inception of canning at Rivers Inlet in 1881 and for half a century following, virtually every able-bodied Haisla made part of his living off commercial fishing."

Tug towing canoes to the cannery, 1914

A Home for Children

It was the mass exit of the entire village to the canneries that prompted George Raley, the new missionary, to build a home for the children. The children had traditionally accompanied their parents to Rivers Inlet, but in the opinion of the missionary, the transient life was not good for the young. A proper education under such conditions was simply not possible. Both Rev. Raley and his wife were determined to open a home for native children in the village so that they could attend school on a regular basis, and also keep them under the constant influence of a Christian teacher.

Children outside the Kitamaat Home

The idea of a home for children was not a new one. Indeed, some already existed in villages where money had allowed. Christian homes, operated by missionaries were not unlike boarding schools. As many children as possible lived at the school. Those who could not be accommodated, due to a lack of space, attended the day school. Many missionaries considered this method of schooling as the only worthwhile one. Martha Walker, who arrived in 1898, explained in a church magazine her decision to take up residence at Kitamaat. "Kitamaat has a home, and I believe that the most satisfactory work that can be done for the Indian people is in training the children in a residential home."

In mid-January 1894, despite the cold and snowy conditions, the first Kitamaat home was built. The community donated both lumber and time to its construction. Mrs. Raley prepared meals for 22 children, using the food supplied by the parents. Each child was expected to bring their own bedding and dishes, as extra money for materials was not available. The first school accommodated both boys and girls, ranging in age from eight to sixteen. The boys slept at the back of the schoolroom behind a partition and the girls at the mission house.

In 1895, the Women's Missionary Society of Ontario gave Reverend Raley a grant of $200.00. Donations of cash and materials were essential to maintain mission activities at Kitamaat.

In all of the isolated spots along the coast where the missionaries worked, there was a reliance on the generosity of concerned outsiders. It was the job of the missionary to canvass groups and individuals for financial assistance. It wasn't an easy task, especially when there were so many worthwhile causes in search of extra money. Rev. Raley was particularly adept at raising funds because donations became more abundant.

The Women's Missionary Society was a group operating out of Toronto, and in the years that followed, they developed a special relationship with the Haisla village at Kitamaat. Rev. Raley kept the members in the city of Toronto informed of the developments that their financial support allowed. So it was that Kitamaat became an example to these women of the changing lifestyle of the B.C. natives.

That first $200.00 went towards additions to the home, so that in 1896 there was a building of four rooms, kitchen, girls' living room, storeroom and a room for the full-time teacher. In 1896, Miss Long arrived as the first matron of the Kitamaat home. In a letter written to the Women's Mission Society she describes those four rooms, "The room was quite pleasant in the morning when the sun was shining, but when it rained, which was very often, streams of water ran all over the floor and I had to keep two or three little girls mopping it up. The kitchen was large but very rough, just one thickness of boards which had shrunk so much that they were nearly a quarter of an inch apart. We really suffered with cold the first two winters. It was impossible to teach the girls very much about housekeeping in such a building but I did my best, always hoping for a better time."

Martha Elizabeth Jane Walker. This picture was taken in 1878 when she was 18 years old. Miss Walker later married George Anderson, the first homesteader in the valley.

Girls outside the Kitamaat Home in 1902. First published in a Christmas booklet advertised in the Na Na Kwa in 1902.

A better time came in the latter months of 1897 in the form of another cash donation from the Women's Missionary Society. The money was used to build a new children's home. Construction began immediately and when completed the building boasted a teacher's room, sewing room, a large dormitory that slept 30 girls, a kitchen and storeroom. Rev. Raley wrote, "The people have done a great deal of work. The building is entirely wood with the exception of four chimneys which are terra cotta pipe. There are

34 windows and two fire escapes leading from the dormitory." At a later date Raley further noted, with pride, that "a civil engineer, a cannery manager and a sawmill manager had all estimated the building in its present position worth, at a low figure, between $2,000.00 and $2,500.00."

Miss Elizabeth E. Long and her class.

The First Christmas Meal

"The day was quite mild, snow fell in the evening. The older girls assisted with the choir. The church looked very pretty in its Christmas dress of evergreens. After Church came dinner. This was the first meal in the new home. Of course, I had an extra good dinner for the children. It consisted of canned roast beef, vegetables and a big plum pudding made by Mrs. Raley, also nuts and home made candy for dessert. At 4 o'clock we gave the old people soup, bread and tea in the school. Then the children furnished entertainment, which consisted of choruses, quartets, recitation and calistenics." Christmas dinner as described by Miss Long, was indicative of the success of the new home.

Where the girls once slept in two-storey bunks, the new building had comfortable double beds. Boys' dormitories were added and the home had everything for which Rev. Raley and Matron Long could have asked. In that same year, however, the Women's Missionary Society who practically owned the building requested that the boys be phased out of the Kitamaat home. In the year following the decree, the Women's Missionary Society took over the management of the home relieving Rev. Raley of that responsibility. This meant Raley and his co-workers could continue at the home and school, but they would be under the direction of the Society.

Disaster struck on the 20th of May, 1906, when the home was destroyed by fire. It was Sunday morning and the mission church was just filling up with worshippers for the regular service. The usual routine was interrupted when the home watchman cried out "Fire". The church emptied quickly as people raced to the foot of the hill where the home was built, and saw a mass of smoke and flame. Moveable items were taken out while it was still safe but within 20 minutes following the first cries of fire, the roof of the Kitamaat Home collapsed.

The new Elizabeth Long Memorial Home and Day School built following
the 1906 fire. Courtesy of the Provincial Archives PABC#28931

-RULES.-

KITAMAAT HOME.

—1897-8.—

GENERAL RULES!

1. Cheerful obedience at all times.
2. Strict order must be maintained.
3. All must strive to learn the ENGLISH LANGUAGE as quickly as possible; only English will be allowed during meals and sewing school. Girls must speak up, and answer promptly.
4. All doors must be shut quietly.
5. No girls can carry matches or touch the lamps when lighted.
6. No girls can go into the town without leave.
7. No one can go to the spring for water after tea.
8. Slop-pails must not be allowed to overflow.
9. No talking allowed, in bed.
10. There must be no talking, or looking around in church.

SPECIAL RULES -

COOKS

1. Cooks must get up when the first bell is rung in the morning.
2. The water must be changed on the salt fish without fail every morning after breakfast.
3. Bread must be set on Monday and Thursday in the afternoon after tea; and put in tins ready for the oven on Tuesday and Friday before breakfast.
4. Pancakes must be set on Wednesday morning before breakfast.
5. The last cook will be responsible for all the dishes.
6. Cooks must see that the wood-box and water pails are kept filled.

SEWING ROOM GIRL

1. Sweep the room three times a day.
2. Keep up the fires.
3. See all shawls are hung upon right pets.

BEDROOM GIRLS

1. Rooms must be swept with the doors shut.
2. Bedroom girls will sweep the hall and porch also the stairs every day.

SCHOOLROOM

1. School books and slates must be kept in proper places.
2. Girls must go into school when the second bell begins to ring.

Rev. G. H. Raley *principle*
Miss Long *matron*
Mr. Anderson *teacher*

Once again, the Women's Missionary Society donated funds for reconstruction. Miss Long left Kitamaat due to ill health and in her honour the building was named, the "Elizabeth Long Memorial Home". Boys were once again admitted and after six years of exclusion, both parents and children were pleased at the Society's change of heart.

It was around this time that the first government-funded day school was built at the village, thus making education a reality for all the children. By the early 1900's boys of 12 and over were being sent to Coqualeetza in Sardis, B.C. for higher education. It is reported in the book *Living Bells*, a book about mission schools in British Columbia, that there were nine boys from Kitamaat at the school: Able Ross, Matt Wilson, Joseph Grant, Thomas Amos, Edward Gray, Paul Tate, Robert Stewart, Albert Starr and Chris Walker.

Health and Education Prosper

In 1914 the first registered nurse, Miss Alton, arrived at the Kitamaat Mission. She assumed responsibility for the Elizabeth Long Memorial Home and the health of the village. A nurse was a needed addition to the growing population. For many years the village inhabitants had relied on the occasional visits of a doctor stationed at Port Simpson. A story printed in a 1906 issue of the Na Na Kwa related the difficulties of using unproven home remedies. "Joseph Williams while at camp this spring caught cold in a cut finger; a friend of his had a bottle containing carbolic acid, which she suggested would be good to use. Instead of diluting the acid she poured the quantity on the finger with the result that it became like a charred stick. He came to Kitamaat to see the missionary about it and was advised to lose no time in seeing a doctor. He was persuaded to go to Port Simpson. Joseph returned with his hand well healed."

A few years later, around 1917, the missionaries began summer camps for the schoolchildren. The outdoor camp was a compensation for the girls who missed the summer months at the canneries at Rivers Inlet. It was the opinion of the missionaries that the life at Rivers Inlet for teenagers was too permissive and too dangerous for the safety of little ones. For this reason official summer holidays never began until the adults had returned home from the canneries.

On June 10, 1925 the Kitamaat school became the responsibility of the United Church of Canada. The Elizabeth Long Memorial Home lost Nurse Alton, and Miss Dark who had been matron for a number of years. The next few years' changes were frequent in the Home and in the school teaching staff. All of the children from the Home and from the village attended school daily. Since all the older boys and many of the older girls had been attending Coqualeetza, the shear physical work in the Home was much heavier. The little children under 12 couldn't help with much of the workload, and housekeeping in the 1920s was truly hard labour.

The Home closed in the spring of 1941 just three or four years after Kitamaat had celebrated the 60th anniversary of Charlie Amos' first appeal for a teacher. It was replaced by a school built by the provincial government.

George Raley — A Newspaper — A Temperance Society

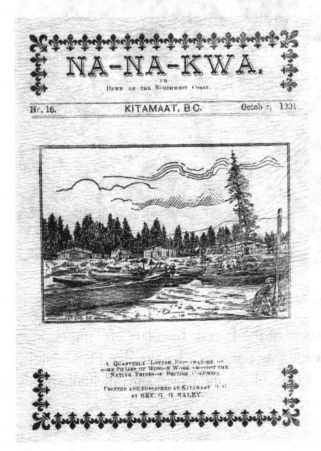

During his time in Kitamaat, George Raley edited a small newspaper, *Na-Na-Kwa*, and promoted a Temperance Society. The newsletter printed and edited under Raley's tutelage, had served as the communication between the Kitamaat Mission and the Women's Society in Ontario, as well as a forum for all of the missions on the Pacific coast. His newsletter included an interesting combination of current events and folklore. *Na-Na-Kwa*, spanning seven years of Kitamaat history, remains an excellent document of life at the turn of the century in Kitamaat.

Both trade and consumption of liquor had always been a concern for the missions along the British Columbian coast, and a Temperance Society was formed by the people of Kitamaat Village. The Society was affiliated with a larger organization called the Royal Templars of Temperance. To become a member of the group, which held weekly meetings, was not an easy matter. One had to sign a declaration that insisted on a belief in, "the almighty God, as revealed in the sacred scriptures, abstinence, and a belief that an interest in humanity and rightness demands the destruction of the traffic in strong drink." A member in good standing did not frequent places where liquors were sold, nor could they give or sell to others any alcoholic beverages. The declaration of temperance was signed and witnessed, and in the case of unfaithfulness to the creed, the member was openly denounced by the other members.

Reverend G.H. Raley on his return visit to Kitamaat in
1957. Courtesy of the Northern Sentinel Press

A meeting hall was built by the members of the Royal Templars of Temperance. The building was 35 by 25 feet. All work was done free by the Templars. Nails, windows, doors and paint were bought from subscription fees and all lumber was obtained by trading logs for cut wood.

On Thursday, December 28, 1898 a newly built Temperance Hall was formally opened at Kitamaat by Reverend Raley and officers of the Temperance Society. The whole village was invited to the opening feast to commemorate the event. No records were made of the exact success of the society, but it can be said that it exerted some pressure on the growing community.

Missionaries would continue to play a considerable role in the life of Kitamaat during the early part of the 20th century but for the most part the work was completed. The Christian following had grown with Reverend Raley who was remembered by the old-timers from Kitamaat Village. John and Mary Hall were questioned in 1971 about the passage of their 80 years at the Village and they remember with amazement the adjustments made by their people. They recall with considerable affection both Reverend Raley and the first school. Mary in particular remembers that "we all used to go to church in the old days. We got ready for that day and we didn't do any work. Everyone went to the service. Now they don't care much for that but we never missed in our day."

The church brought much change to the Haisla way of life, but the early years of the new century would bring additional change.

Kitamaat, ca 1908. The building with the spire is the
Royal Temple of Temperance build by the Templars in 1898.
Courtesy of the Provincial Archives PABC#61071

Swanson Bay in 1909. The pulp and saw mill at Swanson Bay
ushered in a period of prosperity at Kitamaat.

Town II
The Northern Terminus

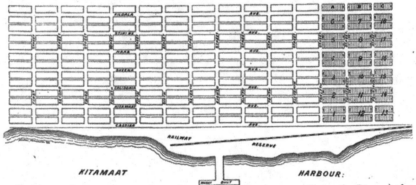

1906 Flyer distributed in Vancouver, British Columbia

Chapter IV
Commerce & Prosperity

Swanson Bay Pulp Centre

In 1903 a lease was granted to a company for 84,180 acres of crown timber near Swanson Bay, near the mouth of the Douglas Channel. Four years passed, and still there was no sign of logging or any definite plans for the manufacture of pulp and paper. Finally, the Canadian Pacific Pulp Company Limited took over the lease and by mid-summer of 1907 a sawmill had been built. When regular pulp production began in 1909, the mill's capacity was reported as 25 tons per day.

Kitamaat Village in winter, 1909

31

Swanson Bay grew and became a port of call for many Canadian steamship companies. A small town was built and by 1918 there was a populace of 500. The inhabitants, according to the Victoria Times of July 26, 1918, "all lived in the company's houses, all eat the company's food, enjoy themselves in the company's recreation hall." The article continues, "they are treated very well, provided with all modern luxuries, except automobiles, and the only reason for that is that there is no room to drive without falling off into the sea."

Kitamaat had an interesting relationship with Swanson Bay. The natives were proficient hand loggers. They felled the timber growing along the channel into the sea, then boomed and towed the logs to Swanson Bay. The resulting profit ushered in a period of prosperity which Gordon Robinson claims, "was unequalled even during the height of construction of the present day Alcan smelter." Robinson goes on, "the profit from this logging operation was used by the Haisla for the construction of very large houses still seen in the village. The Haisla were also able to buy gas boats which further revolutionized the life of the people, for these gas boats made transportation much easier than formerly." The pulp mill was also a boon to the increasing number of settlers now coming into the Kitimat Valley.

Around 1935 Swanson Bay was shut down and this limited the amount of cash coming to the village. Now the logs had to be transported at great cost to Ocean Falls, making for reduced profits.

Prospecting and Mining at Kitamaat

The dream of finding hidden riches particularly gold brought a steady trickle of prospectors into the Kitimat Valley. The substantial finds in other areas of the province — the Klondike and Placer goldfields — provided fuel to the prospecting fever. In 1899 the annual reports from the Ministry of Mines recorded discoveries in the Kitimat Arm. It listed four principal claims: Copper Queen, Mighty Dollar, Kitamaat Gem and Golden Crown.

The Golden Crown claim owned by Messrs. Steele and Dunn proved in future years to be the most profitable of these four. In the summer of 1898 Steele and Dunn spent about six weeks in the Kitamaat neighbourhood employing local natives in the surveying and prospecting work. John Dunn wrote that "we have prospected up to the head of several creeks that empty into the Kitamaat and have found some very favourable indication of there being a mineral bearing belt running through the country."

That first summer for the two prospectors was filled with adventures. In their daily treks from the main camp at the village they often tangled with wild animals. One such incident was particularly noteworthy and Mr. Steel wrote: "Half-way up our dog treed a cub. John Bolton, our Indian packer, killed it and got some fresh meat. The dog struck ahead of us again and in a few minutes came back with a female bear close behind him. The bear came within 15 yards and John at once dropped the shotgun, pulled the revolver as we had no rifle, and fired at the bear striking her in the neck. This did not seem to have much effect and she shook her head and ran off down the mountain. But soon she returned. John picked up the shotgun and fired, striking her full in the face, her roar could have been heard a mile away, she pawed her face and tore around for a minute or two." Eventually John managed to put the bear out of her misery but not until six further shots had been fired.

In the summer of 1900 Steel and Dunn met with further adventure and a fatality was only barely avoided. John Dunn wrote about the incident in a letter published in the Na Na Kwa: "After getting through our work on the claims we started up the Kitamaat River, reaching about 15 miles above tide water, when our canoe got caught in a jam and then sunk immediately with all of our baggage. We nearly lost a man in the stern of the canoe. This ended our trip for the present but we intend to give the Kitamaat River another trial."

Sketch of Golden Crown claim from the Na Na Kwa.

Of course prospectors were not the only people to face dangers in the Kitimat Valley, but because their work often forced them to spend long periods of time away from the main camp, the incidence of near tragedy was all the more likely. The work itself was backbreaking. Tools at that time were primitive and safely stripping away the mountainsides took considerable expertise.

In 1901, concerted work was done to open up the Golden Crown camp. With help from Government monies, Steel and Dunn began building a wagon road from the Kitimat Arm to the mineral claim located about four miles inland from the inlet. In the fall of that same year, Reverend Raley took a walk on that new road. He wrote that he was impressed with its excellent condition and the walk in total took him just an hour and a half. The property he reached at the end of the road was the first in the vicinity to yield copper and gold. Steel and Dunn themselves were pleased with the quartz they had extracted from the Golden Crown claim. It was uniformly mineralized and they could only hope they had found a permanent ledge. It was that hope which prompted the men to build a permanent cabin and blacksmith shop at the claim site in preparation for a winter stay. By 1904, the Golden Crown property was being proclaimed as a wealthy site. This proclamation was made during Kitamaat's period of hyper-optimism and the prospecting business was in no way immune from that boom's enthusiasm.

In the spring of 1957, Leon Kirstein, a surveyor for the Aluminum Company of Canada, accidentally came upon the remnants of the Golden Crown claim. There were only a few indications of the once prosperous mining concern. Kirstein found a rotting bridge, probably part of the road, decomposed logs and a 30-foot tunnel. It seems that the project was abandoned in 1909 — in all likelihood because it ceased to be profitable. In 1928, the Calibre Exploration Company re-staked that same spot near Wahtl Creek. However, no work was done and that company later went into liquidation.

In the late 1960's when Eurocan made preparations to push a logging road into the Raley Creek Valley, the crew came upon a set of prospector's tools. There were hand-forged hammers, chisels, picks and scrapers. It is difficult to determine to whom they belonged to, but a jar, registering the year 1902, suggested they were probably owned by one of the early pioneer prospectors. Each tool was stamped "M.P.", the initials of the prospecting team of Mooney & Pettigrew.

These discarded tools are now in the collections of the Kitimat Museum & Archives and are among the few mementoes that are left to recall those who spent years in search of a fortune in the Kitimat Valley. They left as they came for the most part, not much richer, but with a lifetime stock of stories and a recognized place in the pioneer history of this valley.

Railway Fever

The fever began with the surveyors. There were many who crisscrossed the northern regions of British Columbia in the late 1800's and one of them, Charles Horetzky, travelled up into the Kitimat Valley. Horetzky had joined the Canadian Pacific Railway surveys in the mid-1870's. This adventurous and highly competent man was described by Pierre Burton in his book The National Dream as "a strapping giant with brooding eyes and vast black beard." Horetzky had been employed by the Hudson's Bay Company before he was commissioned by the CPR to determine alternate routes to a northern tidewater terminus on the Pacific. Canada was a vast country and it was essential that a railway be built to link the east coast to the west. The Rocky Mountains provided the greatest difficulties for such a project and the CPR was attempting to find a suitable passage for a rail line.

Horetzky and John Macon, a biologist, were to travel through the mountains, then to Fort St. James, and on to the coast. It was Horetzky's plan to find the necessary route through the Rockies. As the two men journeyed, it became clear that this strapping giant had no intentions of following the earlier plans. When they arrived in Fort St. James, the exact centre of British Columbia, Horetzky began to push forward into the west through unknown country and finally to the mouth of the Skeena.

In 1874 Charles Horetzky entered the Kitamaat harbour and although the weather was difficult, he managed to explore the Kitimat Valley. He noted with particular favour the natural features of the valley and adaptability for a harbour at Minnette Bay and a railway terminus. Horetzky catalogued all that he saw in his exploratory mission, and in a report entitled *Some Startling Facts*, Charles Horetzky proclaimed Kitamaat as the best alternative for the terminus. Others were not so impressed. By 1880, Charles Horetzky wrote to Sir Fleming, the chief surveyor, claiming that the Kitimat Valley alternative—the finest valley without exception on the B.C. seaboard—had been overlooked without any assigned reason. In spite of Horetzky's fanatical urgings, Fleming remained unconvinced that Kitamaat was a feasible terminus site.

At this time there were still no definite plans for a rail link, as development was still concentrated in the southern areas of the province. In later years however, a link to the north was deemed necessary. Many surveyors agreed with Horetzky, and with so much optimistic coverage, it was no surprise that when a northern rail line was in the concrete planning stages, Kitamaat became a favoured possibility of surveyors. Inhabitants began to believe that Kitamaat would indeed be the northern terminus for the rail line.

George Anderson, the Kitimat Valley's first homesteader, had a firm belief that Kitamaat would have a special place in B.C.'s future. Elizabeth Anderson Varley in her book *Kitimat My Valley*, wrote of her father's hopes: "Kitimat will one day be the second largest outlet of Canada on the Pacific Coast. Why? Why because there is no other point on the entire coast where the railway can reach a usable port on the sea. It must be by way of the Skeena, then down through this valley to the sea. There is nothing to obstruct deep sea shipping from the Pacific straight up the Douglas Channel; it's deep and clear

Charles Horetzky, railway surveyor: "A strapping giant". Mr. Horetzky presented evidence supporting the location of the CPR terminus at Kitamaat. Courtesy of Ottawa Archives

of obstacles right to the head. Moreover there is a place for a city here . . ." In this George Anderson summed up the hopes and dreams of many of the settlers who were attracted to the valley's potential. Fierce speculation began around Kitamaat—there were fortunes to be made in the railway business and a number of astute entrepreneurs were vying for the railroad rights.

Charles Clifford and The Kitamaat-Omineca and Grand Trunk Railways

In 1900, Mr. Charles Clifford and his associates were given the rights by the Provincial Government to construct a railway from Kitamaat to Hazelton and then on to the Yukon. The Kitamaat-Omineca Railroad, as it was called, precipitated Kitamaat's first real boom. An old-timer from Smithers, Mr. Wiggs O'Neil, wrote of his first impressions of Clifford: "An old gentleman who had been a Hudson's Bay Manager all his life, also a member of the British Columbia Legislature, promoted a railway

company to build from Kitamaat across the Skeena River, and on into the Omineca placer gold diggings. He was a good talker and promoter. He got my stepfather and his wealthy brother in Scotland interested and almost everyone on the north Pacific coast who had a buck to spare, and also several big shots in Victoria."

Clifford was an astute businessman. As early as 1896 he had made applications for land grants in the Kitamaat area and by 1906 the Sun newspaper from Port Essington states that, "C.W.D. Clifford is in Kitamaat looking over his large interests there." Charles Clifford by that time had sold his railway charter to the Grand Trunk Pacific but had managed to secure a great deal of land as well as develop a plan for the new city.

The Grand Trunk Railway was what is called a development railway. Its economic viability lay in the traffic that would result from the opening up of raw wilderness.

Charles William Clifford, Member of the British Columbia Legislature for the Skeena riding and a fierce promoter of Kitamaat for the northern railway terminus. Courtesy of the Provincial Archives PABC#5296

When the Grand Trunk Railway Company purchased the Kitamaat-Omenica charter it suggested to many that construction would begin soon. That transaction provided extra fuel for Clifford as well as for other speculative activity.

In 1904, in anticipation of Kitamaat's bright future, Clifford built a small hotel. It was a two-storey building of seven rooms and a kitchen. Meals were served and it was said that Clifford's hotel did a roaring business in rum.

By 1905, Kitamaat was a bustle of activity. Clifford had completed the layout of the townsite. The new plan consisted of 14 streets and seven avenues laid out in a grid system. The lots were small and highly priced. A Vancouver realty company, B.C. Johnston and Howe, were instructed with marketing these lots. The realtors published a formidable advertisement announcing the sale of lots at Kitamaat. It described the new townsite in glowing terms heralding Kitamaat as "the most feasible terminus for the great railway outlet on the north Pacific coast." The advertisement continued: "Kitamaat has a natural townsite sloping back from the waterfront, it is destined to be one of the most important seaports on the Pacific coast." In concluding the ad, Kitamaat's future was compared to Vancouver's. "Remember, four lots in Vancouver when first put on the market sold for $4,250.00. A portion of them has since been sold at a price showing the four to be worth $110,000, making a gain of a hundred percent per annum during the time. Kitamaat has as bright an outlook today as Vancouver had then."

The Kitamaat Hotel built by C.W. Clifford. It was eventually dismantled in 1916 by George Anderson. Courtesy of the Provincial Archives of British Columbia, PABC #69417

There most certainly was a bright future in store for the town of Kitamaat but the ad was to prove itself premature. When the advertised sale of lots began there had as yet been no definite decision on the location of the rail terminus. Other spots were being considered and Kitamaat still did not have the support of some of the important decision-makers. Nevertheless optimistic pioneers and entrepreneurs, so sure of Kitamaat's great future, went ahead with development plans.

C.W. Clifford's commercialism of the Kitimat Valley was typical of B.C.'s boom era. His proclaimed skill as a promoter made for further speculation in the Kitamaat vicinity. His confidence had an infectious quality, so it was not surprising that the mission workers, settlers and prospective business people were convinced of Clifford's second sight.

The bubble burst in 1907 when Kaien Island or Prince Rupert as it is now called, was chosen as the railway terminus. Many factors were involved in that momentous decision to bypass Kitamaat, and ironically, one of them was the excessively high prices for land in the area. It seems that the lots sold by B.C. Johnston and Howe at Kitamaat had been purchased by speculators who were intent on fulfilling the promises made to them in the realtors' advertisement, and consequently, set a resale price that was simply too high.

Many people at Kitamaat thought the Kaien Island spot was impractical because of the difficulties of laying rail through the narrow Skeena Valley. But despite the favourable opinions of navigators, railroad engineers and 50 years of survey reports, Kitamaat was bypassed and the route to Prince Rupert was chosen. It was a blow for both the inhabitants of Kitamaat and for the speculators who had put hopes and cash into the railway dream.

There was no instant evacuation of the area following the official decision but, as the years passed, things slowed down considerably in the Kitimat Valley. However, provincial government field staff continued to investigate the Valley's potential. Herbert Naden Clague articled with John Hirsch, a B.C. Licensed Surveyor. Hirsch had surveyed the valley for the government in the years previous to Clague. Clague's government-financed surveys of 1910 and 1911 assessed the valley's suitability for agricultural and other purposes and provided sketch plans of the mountain country. In letters to his fiancée Clague writes of the hardships faced: "The early part of last week we commenced moving our grub and outfits up the Kitamaat River. It is a hard trip up the river and a pretty dangerous one in places. I am glad I am not nervous. We certainly had an exciting trip. We smashed two paddles, lost one oar, one pike pole, some stove pipe, one large bread pan and a few pounds in weight." Neville F. Townsend, one of Clague's surveyors, took a number of images of the summer survey in 1911.

The survey crew of N.F. Townsend going
up the Kitimat River, August 1911.

Herbert Naden Clague, Government
Surveyor in Kitamaat in 1910. Clague
Mountain is named after him.

The Pioneers

When it was rumoured that Kitamaat would be the terminus for the Grand Trunk
Railway, it became a feasible place for settlement. Many people moved into the area to
begin work on ranches, farms and other such enterprises. The first settler was George
Anderson. He had come to Kitamaat from Ontario in the early 1890's to take up
the position of teacher at the mission school. Anderson and his bride, Cora, were
committed to mission work at Kitamaat. George Anderson's daughter, Elizabeth,
wrote: "Their single interest was to serve God, and they were armed with missionary
fervour and wonderment at the new world in which they found themselves." They
worked with great cause, became fast friends with the natives, and found happiness in
the Kitimat Valley.

In 1898, George Anderson resigned from the mission. His wife had passed away
three years earlier and their two children were now living with grandparents in Quebec.
George had put in a good five years of work at the mission and now became Kitimat
Valley's first pioneer homesteader. Two years prior to his resignation, George had
begun to clear a section of land across the water from the village for future settlement.

Janice Beck

The Haisla called this land "Kouwthpega" and so that was the name by which George Anderson's new ranch was known.

In 1898, the Mission acquired a new worker, Miss Martha Walker. Although she was enthusiastic about her missionary work, in the summer of 1900 she too resigned her post to marry George. The union made the start of a successful ranch and farm that would provide a good example for their future neighbours.

George had shipped in farm equipment, horses, cows, and a pig on a steamer and had hopes of making a substantial living from livestock rearing. That first year of marriage was a busy one for George and Martha. There was hay to be put up and the large vegetable garden needed constant care. The animals had to be tended and, of course, there were the cooking and cleaning chores. Women's work, as the adage goes, is never done, and for Martha the days were never long enough. She was a strong and sturdy sort and by all accounts was well suited to the life of a pioneer wife. The long winters and the year-round separation from friends and family added to the difficulties of the pioneer. It was always these same difficult circumstances that greeted each and every settler to the Kitimat Valley. If one were willing to work with energy and perseverance, a reasonable living and rewarding existence were assured.

Of great importance to the settlers in the Kitimat Valley, or in any other isolated spot, was their accessibility to the outside world. Mail was often their only link to relatives and the only means of obtaining supplies necessary for their lonely existence. In 1900, Rev. Raley had been successful in persuading the government to provide Kitamaat with a registered post office. This meant there was always a guarantee

At the Anderson's ranch: Elizabeth with her mother, Martha and baby brother, Bert. George Anderson is on the far right.

of a monthly boat arriving at Kitamaat. One could order necessary articles from mail order houses and after the usual two-month wait, machinery, fabric, tools and such could be picked up at the post office. Travel to the south was by no means easy, but a passage to Victoria could always be arranged. While the railway boom was in full swing, a weekly steamer service brought the mail in regularly and travel to and from Kitamaat was extremely easy.

Barney Mulvaney's dog team carrying a load of mail from Kitamaat
in 1910. Winter hardship on the mail run to Hazelton.

Mail from the interior came in by dog team in the winter and by foot in the summer.
The mail carriers of that route had tales of hardship that could fill a book. The added
bulk of mail during the Grand Trunk Railway days made for frequent trips over the
often treacherous trail from Hazelton.

Following the boom, Elizabeth Anderson Varley writes that, "Weekly steamer
service ceased and travel in and out of Kitamaat became more and more difficult.
The C.P.R. dropped the franchise for the mail run and it was eventually picked up
by a bright new company—the Union Steamship Company of B.C.—on a promise
of twelve trips a year." She continues, "Kitamaat was a nuisance call for both the
company and men, it added an extra eight hours or more on their regular schedule
from Victoria to Prince Rupert. So they simply passed us up when the detour was too
inconvenient."

Social life was another concern for those who had settled in the Valley. The farms
themselves were miles apart and all the settlers were a fair distance from the Village,
store and Mission. If weather permitted, they would make the trek to the Village or to
a neighbour's on Sunday; but during winter it was most often an impossible venture.
The Village itself had little to offer in the way of entertainment. The hotel built by
Clifford had not operated for long and the ladies at the Mission House were often too
busy to chat for any great length of time.

For the most part, the ranchers and other settlers derived their pleasure from their work. Gardens in the summertime were wonders to the eye and the fruit trees, carefully cultivated, brought satisfaction.

The community of settlers was a close-knit one. George and Martha Anderson helped many of their neighbours during the difficult initial stages of settling in, and the newcomers in repayment when time allowed, would often lend a hand at Kouwthpega Ranch.

The pioneers of the Kitimat Valley were a diverse bunch. There were a number of European immigrants that lived around Kitamaat for a short time. David Cordelia, a Finn, was one. He lived at Cranberry Flats with a Haisla woman and by all accounts, the couple led an extremely solitary life. Alex Badetch, originally from Russia, also lived in the Valley for a short time, but little is known of his life there. Other people who moved into the Valley to begin a new life met with tragedy. Jim Dinner, who Elizabeth Anderson remembers as an educated man, built a log house west of the Anderson ranch. Some time after 1904, Dinner was killed by a falling tree. He had been a regular visitor to the Anderson home and George had often relied on his help.

Logging camp on the west side of Douglas Channel, 1939.

Mr. and Mrs. Keppler and their two children had a homestead in the Valley. The Kepplers suffered a marital breakup and Mrs. Keppler left the Valley. The pioneer life may have been too great a strain. Their cabin was vacated and the Kepplers short stay ended. Another man, Mr. Daton, drowned in the Kitamaat River. He left behind him a piece of half-cleared land and a wife. She stayed with the Andersons until a passage out could be arranged. Another family that was the recipient of the Andersons' hospitality was the Worthings. Floyd and May Worthing along with their son Arnold arrived in Kitamaat in 1913. They stayed with the Andersons for a few days. One year later they had built their own log cabin. The following summer, the house burned down and the Worthings lost everything. In 1916 Mr. Worthing left to join the Army as had many of the men in the

Valley. Most of those who left to enlist never did return and Mr. Worthing was among that set. By 1920, only four families and a logging camp were left: George Anderson, Rudolf Braun, Charles Carlson and Charlie Moore.

The logging operation was run by Bob Mitchell and Frank Hallett. The property they worked was located near the present settling ponds of the Eurocan Mill. When the First World War broke out in 1914, the operation was significantly expanded. They worked further down the Douglas Channel logging spruce for war material.

George and Martha Anderson, their children all grown up and their livestock depleted, retired to Sardis, leaving the Kitimat Valley for good in 1926. Mr. Anderson had lived in Kitamaat for more than 30 years. He had made a living selling beef, milk and butter to the Village population. His success as a pioneer and his historical importance to the making of British Columbia is a matter of record.

In 1937, James and Edna Alexander came to Kitamaat after hearing of the great farming potential of the Valley. They brought their children, Enoch, Kenneth, Ronald, Wilburt, Celia and Lloyd. Alice and Ted Alexander were born in Kitamaat in 1938 and 1939. The Alexanders knew the Brauns, Moores, Hans Hanson, and Charlie Carlson. These were the few settlers left in the Valley at that time.

In 1940, a flood destroyed the old Anderson barn. Mr. Alexander built a new one but by 1941 it was clear that it was impossible to sell produce from such a remote location when small mills and mining operations had all shut down in the 1930s. The Alexanders left the valley in July 1941.

Charlie Moore was one of the earliest settlers. He first arrived in the valley in 1900. Some say he and a few other men had rowed all the way from Victoria in a sixteen-foot boat. Eventually he settled near the present-day sand hill. Moore Creek in Kitimat is named after him.

Charlie and his first wife, Lizzie, had two children. Lizzie, who suffered from cancer, died in 1919. The young children went to live with relatives. Moore stayed on in the Valley and some rumours have it that he left Kitamaat but once in all his years there. That was in 1925 when he single-handedly rowed to Prince Rupert and back. In 1927 Mr. Moore married Miss Theodora Anderson (no relation to George Anderson) who was a matron of the girls' home at the Village.

Charles and Theodora Moore loading hay. Their cattle were
brought up from the colony farm Essondale.

Ted and Alice Alexander in front of the Anderson House, 1939.

James Harris Alexander with his children, from left to right,
Ken, Ron, Lloyd, Wilburt, Celia and Alice.

Moore made his living at first by trapping and later his farm supplied most of his needs. He died in 1943, one of the last of the early settlers to leave the Valley. Mrs. Moore later sold her property to Alcan in the early 50's.

One of the more off-beat and interesting characters to settle at Kitamaat was Charlie Carlson. He told Rita Rogerson about the circumstance of his first visit to Kitamaat: "Two other chaps and I started in a sailing boat, prospecting and trapping as we went along. We found the trapping good along the Douglas Channel, so we stayed there until we found our food running low. By studying an old map we had with us, we saw the nearest place to buy food would be Hartley Bay. At Hartley Bay we found a deserted place except for a one-eyed Indian and a sick preacher. The missionary told us to go on to Kitamaat, that there were people and a store."

In 1914, Charlie filed a homestead of 60 acres and bought an adjoining 40-acre lot. Later he built a decent home. Carlson said, "After living in shacks so long, I felt I deserved a decent house, with plenty of room for my bachelor friends. Besides if the right girl ever showed up, well, I'd have the house; only that right girl never did show up."

In 1929, Carlson sold his livestock and spent every summer fishing on the boat he had built. His free-wheeling bachelor lifestyle did not go over well with the other pioneers nor the mission staff, so Carlson spent most of his time with transient trappers and loggers who passed through Kitamaat.

In 1944, Carlson left Kitamaat for good. In 1951, Charlie told a reporter from the North West Digest, "The reason we stayed in Kitamaat so long was that we thought a railway would come in sooner or later and a town would grow. Well, when she died little by little instead, naturally we lost heart. I'm glad to see Kitimat come into its own; it seems like a dream come true."

Charlie Carlson, 1939

The house that Charlie Carlson built. Photo taken in 1958.

Bringing supplies into Kitamaat. Arnold Worthing at right, 1914.

The Braun Farm

Rudolf Braun was a native of Germany. He left Hamburg as a young man to join one of the Atlantic steamship companies. In 1912, while in Montreal, Rudolf heard that the government planned to open up the most westerly province for settlement. He travelled across the country and settled on a piece of land on Minnette Bay. His enterprise called the Minnette Ranch started slowly. In 1914, when the First World War broke out and many of the single men left Kitamaat, Rudolf stayed on. With long days and great effort, he cleared the land and built a one-room home. He bought some livestock and grazed about 30 head of cattle. For almost ten years Rudolf lived entirely alone. But in 1923 he married a young woman from Germany with whom he had been corresponding for a number of years. When Martha arrived, a big new house was built single-handedly and in that same year Christel, their first child was born. Four sisters followed her, so there were plenty of helping hands at the Braun Farm.

Rudolf was industrious and ambitious and these attributes made for successful farming. Much of the farm produce, milk, and butter were sold to logging outfits along the Channel. Unlike the Andersons, Rudolf preferred not to sell to the Village and his boat called the Minnette made regular trips to the isolated logging camps.

The farm had a large barn and a huge garden and Christel recalled that the summer months were very busy, and there was no time for visiting neighbours. The only real holiday of the year was May 24th, Victoria Day. The family would travel by boat to the Village and partake in the festivities. Mrs. Braun especially enjoyed the chance to visit with the other women and catch up on the general news. The children would compete in sports contests and listen to the very proficient Village band. As the girls grew up, schooling became a problem. In 1932, it was decided that the young girls and their mother would spend the winters in Prince Rupert so a proper education would be assured. Rudolf, used to the hard and lonely winters of his bachelor days, was more than able to handle the farm and livestock alone. In the spring the family would be reunited, and the months of heavy labour would begin.

After five years of this arrangement, life at the Braun farm changed dramatically. One early morning around seven while Martha was baking the week's bread supply, a fire started in the chimney. There was nothing that could be done to stop the destructive flames and the family lost all their belongings, save for the bedding and the freshly baked bread. The only shelter available was the big barn, and the family was forced to set up camp with the livestock. Like the Worthings who lost their home in a fire years earlier, the Brauns decided not to start again from scratch.

In about 1939, the Brauns left Kitamaat for good. Years later Rudolf published a small book of poems. Many of the verses spoke of his years at the Minnette Ranch and, at first reading it is obvious that those times were happy ones. In 1956, at the age of 69 Rudolf passed away. He left behind his gentle poems and remnants of a beautiful farm at Kitamaat.

The house built by Rudolf Braun at Minnette Bay in Kitamaat, circa 1925.

This period in Kitamaat's history is at once exciting and sad. Exciting, in that families such as the Andersons, Brauns and Moores had a great deal of success in their individual ventures. Sad, in that others were more prone to discover the harsh realities of life in the Valley. By 1945, the last of the pioneers had left the area—some desolate, their dreams smashed when the development they had anticipated did not materialize. Yet, others, such as Martha and George Anderson left, having spent a full life rearing a family and a farm to be proud of.

Pioneering began anew — a new town called Kitimat was to be built and the natural potential of the Valley heralded by so many for over 100 years would finally develop.

Kitimat Valley
"Minnette Ranch"

By Rudolf Braun

The MINNETTE RANCH, my Homestead
I named, to accord,
As located on the shore of Minnette Bay:
Minnette Bay being the terminal of a mighty fjord,
On the B.C. Coast, permit me to say:
Minnette Bay, also being the terminal of a roomy vale,
Geographically known as the Kitimat Valley:
The myriads of fertile acres acclaimed by that dale,
Lured in the first place my ego to sally,

Years ago, to be exact it was Nineteen-Twelve,
I concluded, it's time to cease to roam;
Homesick, so I was determined to delve,
And acquire a home of my own:
With an ingrained desire, for a farm and a home,
Thus I spy'd through many a nooks and alley;
Bu during all my ramble, found no paragon,
So I chose the prospective Kitimat Valley.

The Braun's barn was built with the help of the Haisla from Kitamaat Village, ca. 1937.

With an axe, and a saw and ample pep and brawn,
I soon reclaimed some of that virgin land;
My days, usually started at dawn,
Thus I steamed ahead all my ego could stand:
Persevere and succeed, was my motto indeed,
So with me there was no dilly dally;
Thus I soon built up, and acquired a home,
In the prospective Kitimat Valley.

I acquired some pigs, and horses and chicks,
And cows to have spread on the bread;
Thus there was always something to fix,
So I kept tilling and toiling from early till late:
There was no time to loiter, ramble, or roam,

But in spite of, I kept cheerfully singing "O Malley;"
As perseveringly, I hewed out a home
In the prospective Kitimat Valley.

But all work and no play, makes Jack a dull boy,
As up to then I trod through Life's journey alone;
So I acquired a pretty maid, to share in sorrow and joy,
And to enliven my lonely Kitimat Home.
Thus my mate and I, shared in toil and joy;
And raised in addition to cattle and chicks;
Also five rosy-cheeked Maidens sturdy and coy;
Who will some day be good partners for Harry and
Dicks.

The family of Rudolf and Martha Braun "Smiling Greetings from Kitamaat".

Thus we toiled and dined, which we did not mind,
And tending to our cows was our main occupation;
But fate to us was rather ill inclined,
Which may befall individuals, or a nation:
It seemed bad luck was for us destined;
As our Kitimat abode was razed by conflagration;
Let me tell you, it's sure no joke,
To see many years of toil going up in smoke.

Glory to him, who takes loss with a cheerful grin,
Is a very good phrase to keep in mind;
But Kitimat turned into a place dreary and dim,
With little enticement left behind:
Some obstacles were acute, with markets far remote,
And a mail-service! apt to make you whine;

And now, without an abode we stood,
Thus we were obliged with the cows to dine.
With no neighbours, to enthuse our labours,
But the conflagration dealt the final blow;
And our girls need education, was the constant iteration,
So we resolved to abandon that desolate place, and go.

But time goes on, for better or worse,
So also Kitimat Valley was going to learn;
That a prosperous time was going to immerse,
And disperse the gloomy old days in turn:
As a huge Aluminum Industry is going to rear,
So there soon will be many a street and alley,
And of a new Metropolis we are going to hear,
In the prospective Kitimat Valley.

The Kitamaat Silver Band played at many events in Kitamaat and abroad. May
Queen and her attendants (l to r): Annabelle Bolton, Amelia Gray, Hanna
Morrison, Gladys Amos, Grace Bolton, and Marian Wilson, May 24, 1931.

Town III
Aluminum City

Chapter V
The Industrial Connection

In the years following the Second World War, the aluminum industry experienced a period of growth and prosperity. Aluminum, rust resistant and a good conductor of heat, was being used increasingly in the manufacture of aeroplanes, automobiles, and general household articles. The Aluminum Company of Canada prospered and expanded, their product heralded as the metal of the future. It was in the late 1940's that the Aluminum Company of Canada decided that the province of British Columbia offered the best place for a hydro-electric power project as well as a port and smelter site. Alcan, on the invitation of Brian Johnson, B.C. Premier, made extensive explorations in northern B.C. Albert Whitaker, an Alcan executive, wrote of that decision: "In B.C. the political risk was less than other countries. Also, it fitted our part as the dependable Canadian ingot supplier to the world. B.C. seemed preferable to Labrador in regard to the climate and other factors, and was well placed in regard to the Japanese market."

From 1948 to 1950, Alcan surveyed the northern regions, particularly the Nechako/

McMinn, Chief Surveyor of the 1949 B.C. Government survey crew enjoying some of Kitimat's fringe benefits. At this time the Kitimat Alcan Project was still top secret.

Kemano area with concern to the feasibility of a dam and hydro electric project. That same area had been thoroughly explored in the years 1924 to 1928, by Frank Swannell. Swannell had kept tremendous records, photographs, and diaries and, in a detailed report, had indicated the suitability of the area for hydro power. Frederick Knewstubb, the principal engineer for the B.C. Water Rights Branch read Swannell's report and envisioned a plan to locate a dam in the Nechako Canyon. Knewstubb's scheme was shelved due to the War, but his plan was not forgotten.

On December 30th, 1950, a power agreement between the B.C. Government and Alcan was signed. Frederick Knewstubb's dream was to become a reality. A giant power project in the Kemano/Nechako area would provide the necessary electricity for an aluminum smelter at the mouth of the Kitimat River. A townsite was also planned a few miles from the smelter, across the bay from the village of Kitamaat. The 1950 agreement between Alcan and the B.C. Government gave the Aluminum Company a 50-year lease on land and water in that vicinity and also the authority to flood up to 300 square miles of land. It was a momentous occasion for both the government and company. Alcan could now manufacture the metal needed for the growing aluminum market because they have access to the very necessary power source for an aluminum smelter. The government was pleased to help a company that would have a large payroll and eventually construct a brand new town in northern B.C.

The site for the smelter and town was chosen because of its excellent adaptability for a deep-sea port, the availability of level land, and finally, its proximity to the new power development at Kemano 48 miles away. The surveyors of the previous 100 years had not been deluded. Kitimat Valley and the surrounding area had great potential—a potential that would finally be realized.

In 1951, the Aluminum Company of Canada set out its plan in a simple seven-point scheme. Under the heading *How the Alcan Plan Will Work*, was the following:

1. The Nechako River Dam will stop eastward flow.
2. Waters in a drainage area will back up towards the west.
3. A ten mile tunnel through the Cascade Mountains will drop water from drainage area 2,600 feet.
4. A power plant inside a mountain will be capable, ultimately, of developing 1.6 million horsepower.
5. A 48-mile transmission line will carry power to Kitimat.
6. The power will permit electric smelting of 100 million pounds of aluminum per year.
7. The new town of Kitimat will grow into a city of possibly 50,000.

The scheme seemed deceptively simple, but the completion of the power project, smelter and town would take a number of years, thousands of men and incredible expertise. No cost was spared and experts in every field were consulted. The result at Kemano is one of the most awesome revisions of geography ever.

Entrance to the Kemano Power Plant, 1958.

The Kemano Power Project

The possibility of hydro development at Kemano was described by F.T. Matthias, Assistant Manager of the Alcan project as "Nature's Gift". He continued, "And so the stage is set and the Alcan project is putting these natural conditions to work to make aluminum for the hungry markets of the world."

To begin, a dam was built on the Nechako River. The Nechako River for thousands of years drained the lakes of Tweedsmuir Park eastwards. The water flow had to be reversed and a reservoir created to maximize the power potential. The great distance of the location from any city or railroad meant that a natural rock-filled dam would be the most economical method of construction. The engineers would be faced with immense difficulties. The nearest quarry was a few miles away so the rock had to be transported by truck to the site of the Kenney Dam. When the dam was completed it was the third largest rock-filled dam in the world. The reservoir started to fill in October of 1952 and the finger lakes of Tweedsmuir Park became a 120-mile-long reservoir.

Most often hydro-electric power is generated by waterfall. The Alcan project called for a new approach. A tunnel was blasted through a mountain from the reservoir to the powerhouse at Kemano—a distance of ten miles. The tunnel would carry the water in a steady and forceful stream into the generators to produce electricity.

The tunnel called for an even greater amount of earth moving than at the Kenney Dam site. Never before was so much rock moved so quickly. The tunnel crews broke world records as they bored through DuBose Mountain and slowly moved closer to the generators at Kemano. For the workers employed at the Alcan Project, it was a time of strict deadlines. October '53 was the targeted completion date for the tunnel and aluminum production at the Kitimat smelter was set to begin in mid-1954. There was no time to lose. The men who lived in makeshift camps were betting on when they would meet the team working from the opposite end of the tunnel. As the work progressed, the construction camps developed into small towns. The camp on the west side of the reservoir nestled at the base of DuBose Mountain was described by Ken McTaggart of the Globe and Mail as "a community with kids running around, movies, a radio/telephone service by which any point can be reached, and other amenities of so-called civilization. Every item of the camp and for the tunnelling job comes by air or by barge. During the winter, everything and every individual must be flown in over snow-crested mountains."

When the tunnel was finally completed, it was so wide that four cars could stand abreast, and so high that the granite above looked like a darkened sky. By 1954, Alcan had harnessed one-half million horsepower of electricity inside one of the world's largest man-made caves. The powerhouse at Kemano was built inside the mountain and over 2,000 feet below the tunnel. The drop of water from that height into the generators provides immense pressure and a constant flow of electricity.

Crews of Kemano and Horetzky headings meet.

The geographical transformation of the Nechako/Kemano area proved a special test of human intelligence and strength. Both the isolation and hardship that met construction crews and the great geographical obstacles were overcome to realize Alcan's plans. Yet for the naturalists and the few inhabitants of the newly flooded area, the Kemano project was a cause for alarm. Following the government's approval of the Alcan Project, the 79 inhabitants of the proposed dam and reservoir area realized they would have to evacuate. Steve Whip in the Interior News wrote, "When it became obvious that the Kenney Dam would be built, landowners in the area formed an organization with Cyril Shelford heading it. The organization was called the "Ootsa Lake Flood Committee." The government refused to accept any responsibility for negotiating or making sure the landowners got a fair price for their homes and land, so it was up to Alcan and the owners to come to an agreement.

At first Alcan made offers to the respective landowners of $3,000 a quarter section. Emotions were running high and people wanted a fair price for their land. Cyril Shelford told Steve Whip in 1980 that "No one can be paid enough to be pushed out of his home, but we wanted a fair deal. We weren't trying to stop it." Eventually, the Alcan negotiators doubled the offer and when the figure finally reached $15,000 a quarter section, the owners sold and moved out.

The Cheslatta T'en hunted, fished and trapped in the region. Many had large vegetable gardens and herds of cattle and horses for which they grew fields of timothy and clover. Some worked for local sawmills or ranchers and ran trap lines. There were approximately 200 Cheslatta living in four villages and 17 reserves along the Cheslatta River and Cheslatta Lake.

On April 19, 1952, the Cheslatta and the Department of Indian Affairs (D.I.A.) held heated negotiations for four days. D.I.A. officials called the compensation required by the Cheslatta "fantastic and unreasonable" and presented their own offer based on valuations of the land and improvements — excluding traplines — that had been made by Alcan and D.I.A. The return offer to the Cheslatta was substantially less.

On the fourth day, the Cheslatta began to move out, surrendering 1,053 hectares of land - 10 reserves. They relocated during a difficult spring thaw, travelling overland to Grassy Plains, 30 miles to the north, and living in adverse conditions in tents until farms were assigned.

Compensation cheques were received in the summer of 1953, but the people were required to pay for their new land. This was contrary to the surrender documents, which, the Cheslatta believed, called for the complete re-establishment of band members. In March 1993, the Cheslatta accepted $7.4 million from the government as a settlement for inadequate compensation in 1952.

Landowners didn't fight the development as might have been the case today, but many were upset to see the land flooded. Beatrice Carroll, one of the landowners, felt that, "Tweedsmuir Park could have been the world's most beautiful and biggest park."

In 1958, Pierre Burton wrote in Maclean's Magazine, "It is a distressing experience to fly across the daisy chain of lakes that supply the storage water for the power development that produced Kitimat. Tweedsmuir Park has paid the price of progress. Its white sand beaches are gone and from the air each lake seems bordered by a ragged line of decaying brown. In 1955…the flooded area was "no longer suitable for park purposes." The park has been consigned to the past; in return B.C. has been given Kitimat, the town of the future."

Others were concerned that the thousands of dollars worth of timber in the area would be lost to the flood. Les Cox, Conservation Officer at the time, felt that the 80,000 acres of trees should have been logged off by Alcan. The company believed that the flooded timber would eventually rot and float away. That was not the case, and today, the Company and Cheslatta are working to remove the debris. Underwater logging now takes place on the reservoir. Significant amounts of wood are being salvaged by barge using a saw that can cut the trees at their bases.

Electricity produced in the powerhouse at Kemano had to be relayed through the rough terrain by transmission lines to the smelter site at Kitimat. That terrain has been called some of the most rugged and defiant in North America necessitating helicopters for the transportation of the huge aluminum towers to specified sites in the mountain peaks where avalanches were least likely. Because of the difficult terrain and rough winter weather conditions, the line to Kitimat had to be reliable. The strongest transmission cable available was utilized to ensure a continuous flow of electricity. In the event of an interruption, the aluminum smelter, without the constant flow of electricity, would run the risk of losing millions of dollars.

Kemano. The water drops on a sharp incline, 2600 feet to the generators.

The smelter built concurrently with the power project at Kemano, also called for revision of the natural geography. The mud flats, where the smelter was to be built, had to be reinforced with landfill. The natural gravel deposit at the sandhill was what Hugh Meldrum, field auditor for Alcan in 1951, called "Alcan's million dollar baby." It contained an almost unlimited supply of good gravel for fill. A conveyor belt was erected from the gravel hill, four miles up the valley to the plant site. The gravel was then spread as fill for the smelter foundation.

Another important consideration at the Kitimat site was port facilities. Although the Douglas Channel had been called a natural port by the surveyors, the ocean floor needed dredging to give deep-sea vessels enough clearance at the head of Douglas Channel where the Kitimat River had brought down tons of silt and gravel. Many ships would dock at Kitimat. Some would be arriving with the alumina necessary for aluminum ingot production and others would be leaving with a heavy load of ingots.

Dredging was a priority in the first month of work. At Kitimat huge scows dug out the ocean floor. Hugh Meldrum recalled: "From the dredge, a huge 24" pipe on a number of floats went across the marsh. From it, branch lines went out in all directions and day and night, mud, water and rock spewed out into great piles. These were eventually pushed into place by a fleet of bulldozers. Twelve thousand cubic yards were pumped out each day. The noise going through the pipes was terrific and a few days went by before I got accustomed to the sound."

A group of workmen at tower number 106 along the transmission line from Kemano, 1952.

A makeshift camp perched high above the Kemano River valley
provided a stunning view of the wilderness landscape.

Kenney Dam

Here is the sandhill in 1949 as seen by the McMinn Survey Crew. Looking at the sandhill today, it is hard to believe that it once bordered the Kitimat River. The gravel was transported to the smelter site and used in great quantity for the fill.

By 1957, close to 10 million cubic yards of the sandhill had gone into the smelter site foundation and townsite construction. The sandhill that once extended to the Kitimat River had been decreased by an average of 16,000 cubic yards a day! Photograph taken August 14, 1952.

A Completely Twentieth Century Town

Once the power project and the aluminum smelter were complete, permanent employees would be hired. Where would the workforce live? In 1951, there was still no sign of a town. It became Alcan's responsibility to build one. To match the futuristic industrial development, Alcan constructed an equally modern town.

When planning the community, Alcan laid down two basic principles: First, it was not to be a company town; and secondly, the company was to avoid owning permanent housing or business endeavours. It was a huge task to initiate and construct all the amenities that a well-rounded town would need. Alcan didn't "know it all" so they engaged planners at the outset so that nothing would be overlooked.

Clarence Stein, an acknowledged expert in town planning was hired on as consultant. He helped Alcan to make the final decision on the hiring of a planning firm. Whitaker wrote of the decision, "The firm selected as the town planners was Whittlesey and Mayer, a small organization based in New York, but one that gave the task their full attention and I think did a wonderful job at a reasonable rate. One of the larger nationally known town planners in New York wanted a $10,000 fee just to talk to us; and I'm sure they would have cost us far more and I doubt that they would have done as good a job."

The basic purposes of the town as Alcan and Clarence Stein saw them were outlined in the magazine Architectural Forum: "The purpose of Kitimat is the industrial success of the plant. That success will depend on the degree that workers are content, that they like living in Kitimat. Unless the town can attract and hold industrial workers, there will be a continuous turnover and difficulty, interfering with dependable output. The workers must find Kitimat more than temporarily acceptable. They must be enthusiastic about it as a particularly fine place in which to live and bring up their families. It must become the place they want as a homeland, the town they are going to make their own. There is much to contend against in making this possible, including climate, remoteness, strangeness. Men will pioneer for a time in the wilderness for good pay and plenty of good food and a free trip every two months. However, labor turnover is incompatible with an efficient plant, particularly in an industry that requires lengthy training for its workers.

At Kitimat the setting for a good life must be hewn out of the unknown wilderness. Pioneers must become old-timers, bound to Kitimat by enthusiastic love of their town and its unusual qualities."

To attain these goals, the planners Whittlesey and Mayer employed the most modern of urban planning methods. The result is a town that has been called, "Tomorrow's city today", "unique to North America", and completely modern. Kitimat has proven that there are workable alternatives to the ill organized boom towns of the past.

Julian Whittlesey, the junior partner in the planning firm, spent many weeks studying the area of the townsite at Kitimat. On one occasion, while traversing the then heavily wooded area of upper Kitimat, Whittlesey had the misfortune to break his leg. Whitaker recalls, "That didn't deter him. He was an outstanding chap and I think to him can go most of the credit for the fine layout we have of Kitimat today — all the industrial activities west of the river along the railway; the businesses on the intermediate level; and the bulk of the townsite homes and rural business centres and schools and churches on the upper level."

A. Whitaker's impression of Whittlesey's role is an overstatement. Both Mayer and Whittlesey relied heavily on the theories of a century of urban studies as well as a team of experts. Traffic was to be routed through main avenues to bypass the residential streets which were planned in a horseshoe or cul-de-sac fashion. Every home was planned to face the peaceful green open spaces rather than the street and traffic. Finally, the neighbourhood idea was utilized. Homes in a particular neighbourhood would have their own schools and shopping centres.

One of the most important experts called in to help the planners at Kitimat, was Lois Murphy, a sociologist. Murphy felt that the woods and hilly ground should be maintained for their beauty; and suggested plenty of covered areas for children to play under during the rainy months, and special planning by Alcan to provide cultural resources. Murphy was particularly concerned that loneliness at Kitimat and the monotony of a one-industry town would lead to broken marriages, roughhousing and general disquiet.

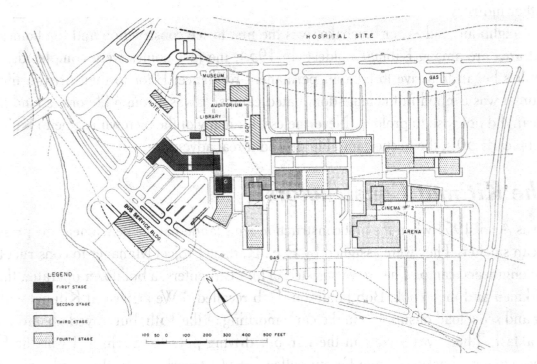

City Centre

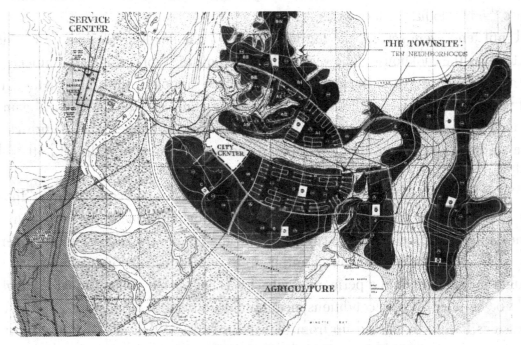

The Town Plan from the *Architectural Forum*, July 1954.

Final plans at Kitimat included tree windbreaks, covered walkways, theatres, a library, a museum, and vast areas of parkland. Mayer and Whittlesey had thought of almost everything and it was now up to Alcan to implement the detailed plans. The town plan itself was developed in stages, it allowed for growth of up to 50,000 people. Alcan intended to have an independent town that in years to come would attract further industry.

Neighbourhood A, or Nechako, was the first to see construction and the homes in that area are among Kitimat's oldest. In 1954, the first homes were completed, and families began to arrive to take up permanent residence. Prior to their arrival, life at Kitimat was centred in the male-dominated camps. It was a rough life of the kind that Alcan did not wish to prolong. Nevertheless, for many of the men who came to Kitimat in the early 50's, the hectic camp life proved a real adventure.

The Kitimat Constructors

It was April 1951 when the first construction crew landed at the beach near the present Alcan smelter. They were assigned by P. E. Radley, Project Manager to construct the first engineers' camp. The crew consisted of four carpenters, a bulldozer operator, three workmen and their cook, Bob Jamieson. Bob recalled, "We arrived at Kitimat with a tug and scow load of supplies in the early morning of the 15th, but stayed aboard until breakfast. There was a crew in the harbour driving piles for a wharf. I was the first ashore to get a bucket of water for our coffee. The first work was to clear and make way for buildings and in this we were helped by some of the Indians who had come from across the bay to have a look at us."

Until tents were set up, the tug was home for the small crew. The first building erected was the cookhouse, followed by the bunkhouses. Work progressed quickly, and when a number of Alcan personnel arrived to have a look at the site on May 11th of that year, the wharf was well on the way to completion and the camp was beginning to take shape. Bob Jamieson remembers that Radley, Whitaker, and Kendrick who were among those first visitors, "were good sports and roughing it didn't bother them at all."

Whitaker wrote of the isolation that faced those first Kitimat constructors: "In those early days the only access to Kitimat or Kemano for individuals was by amphibious planes and helicopter. After the completion of the temporary wharf a steamer service was established between Vancouver and the port— all construction materials had to be brought in by barge until a permanent wharf was completed, when the large freighters could be handled. These conditions meant bulldozers, tools, food, stoves, and all other necessities had to be barged up from the south. Most of the men also arrived in the early days by that same route and it was not until much later that a regular air flight was scheduled into Kitimat."

Construction was moving along at a feverish pace despite the primitive transportation. In July, a larger cookhouse was erected to feed the men who were pouring in by the boatload. A month later, the camp at beachhead was complete and it provided accommodation for 500 men. There were many bunkhouses, tool sheds, offices and a recreation hall. Men arrived in such great numbers that the mess hall was scheduled to feed them in shifts. That following spring, one year after the first crew arrived, a huge cafeteria was complete and it fed 1,800 men daily. Table service gave way to cafeteria line-ups. The men ate heartily to the point that one of them, a man named Morgan, would put away five T-bone steaks in a single sitting.

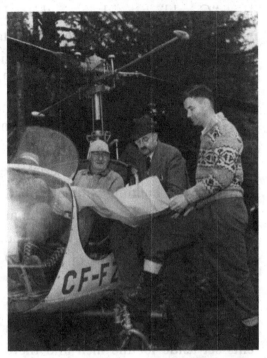

One of the earliest models of helicopter. From left to right: A.W. Whitaker, P.E. Radley, and Jack Kendrick, ca. 1952.

As the project expanded, smaller camps were opened, one at Moore Creek and another at Anderson Creek. The population at the Kitimat camps grew and the wilds of the valley were invaded by machinery.

In those first urgent years of construction, the Kitimat Constructors or K.C.—a consortium of eight construction companies—published a newsletter called Casey Sez. The first issue of "Casey" was passed around to the boys in the bunkhouses in September of '51. It reported one year later that things had greatly improved. "Communications weren't the same as they are now. The road extended only as far as Moore Creek, boats had no schedule. Radio service was limited, ancient movies were shown, almost everybody wore a beard and women was simply a word in the dictionary."

Despite the lack of women, bad weather and bad movies, the men at the camp enthusiastically tried to make the conditions bearable. There were a number of social clubs and a lecture series on photography given by Fred Ryan, Alcan's staff photographer. A discussion group was also initiated. Casey Sez reported: "This group is limited only by the enthusiasm with which it is supported. The discussion group is not a 'longhair' outfit. Don Sullivan says it will discuss anything except the subject which usually occupies 99 percent of the camp conversation!" Could Sullivan have been referring to women?!

Some of the men at the camp spent a lot of their money and time drinking and gambling. Peter Bell who arrived in Kitimat in 1953, spoke to the Ingot of those early days: "Gambling was the main thing. People who were inclined to gamble would come up, take a job such as bull cook and stay up half the night to play cards. And a lot of the bull cooks who didn't play cards did the camp bootlegging. The boat would come in on Friday and the first thing unloaded was the booze. Sometimes by Sunday night the camp would be dry."

Kitimat's reputation as a crazy frontier town was so pronounced it made the pages of the Vancouver Sun. Reporter Alex Young wrote: "A game of blackjack was one of the several games that put some excitement into the hard slugging week of the construction

men who were building Kitimat. Small fortunes are made in the Kitimat gambling tents. We learned from some of the boys that upwards of $30,000 sometimes changes hands in a night close to payday." Gambling at the camp was legal— it all took place in tents set aside for the men and there was no take for the house.

The drinking, wrote the Sun reporter, "was another matter. If it doesn't get out of hand nobody gets too concerned. But if it gets too wild the authorities (three RCMP and 20 Alcan security men) clamp down."

Men arrived by the boatload in the first years of construction on the Project.

Kitimat smelter and Smeltersite, ca. 1954.

The Sun newspaper article entitled, *Rough Tough*, also noted the Delta King steamer high and dry on the beach. Young wrote, "Along the road to the smelter is an amazing site—a huge old sternwheeler. Articles of men's clothing flop in the breeze from the ship's railings." The Delta King was once a riverboat in California but was bought in 1952 by Alcan as a solution to the bunkhouse problem. Whitaker wrote that "the

Delta King was a beautiful old sternwheeler that could carry up to 500 passengers. However, when we finally got it beached, the B.C. Department of Health would not allow accommodation of more than about 250 men. The real benefit we got from the steamer was to supply our temporary hospital with power and augment the early steam plant."

Those first years were rough years at Kitimat. The gambling, drinking and isolation attracted a mixed crowd of Canadians and immigrants. Some had spent years in logging camps or in the Army, so were psychologically equipped for the camp conditions. Others had left wives, children, and loved ones in other parts of the world and were hoping to save up a tidy nest egg. For these men especially, communication to the outside world was essential.

The Delta King in the winter of '55. It had housed 250 men at the height of the construction of Kitimat.

Kitimat's first real post office opened in May 1952 and soon became a favourite place for the boys on Saturday night. The mail was never to be counted on, but usually the Princess Norah arrived with the mail on Saturday evenings. The staff of the post office would sort the mail immediately and then open the wickets to the long queues of men. Replies to the mail had to be written by Monday morning when the Norah made the return trip to Vancouver.

Five months later an airmail service began. The Queen Charlotte Airlines flew mail in regularly, but during the winter months the service was discontinued because of dangerous weather conditions. The winter of 1952 had brought with it some of the worst weather conditions ever recorded. Torrential rains caused

Inside the Delta King. The comfortable quarters were photographed in 1955. Photograph by David S. Boyer © 1956 National Geographic Society

flooding and the huge snowfalls of that year often made work impossible. When spring finally arrived, the men had to contend with the bears who wandered into camp in search of food. Nevertheless, 1952 was truly a year of firsts for Kitimat. It was the year that the bridge over Anderson Creek was finished, and a ferry service began to carry men and machinery to the townsite camp located at the site of the present trailer park.

The first private enterprise, the Bank of Montreal, also began in that special year. It was an essential and well-used building at the smelter site. Business was always very brisk, and on paydays the queues were very long. Many of the men had wives in the south and thousands of dollars in money orders were purchased to send home. The tellers worked in late afternoon and evenings to accommodate the men on shifts. Work at Kitimat continued on a 24-hour basis. The noise of the heavy equipment was constant.

"It is not true, we regret to report that the Delta King is equipped with a cocktail lounge and 50 dancing girls." From *Casey Sez,* May 10, 1952. Cartoon by Al Beaton.

There was a Hudson's Bay store located at Smeltersite. It was one of the last outposts of that Canadian company and rightly so, for Kitimat was truly a place of pioneering. Everything could be bought there, even one's groceries. Business boomed, of course.

At the end of that same year, the first women finally arrived and the first Kitimat baby was born. Old timers recall that it was a race between completion of the hospital and the baby's arrival. The construction crews won and Kathy Cronk, daughter of Kitimat's postmaster, was born on December 4th, the first baby in Kitimat's first hospital.

Lining up for mail at the post office, Feb. 22, 1957.

Most of the women who came to Kitimat were joining their husbands. The married couples lived in a separate area of Smeltersite and in later years would grow in number to necessitate a trailer camp. In 1954, there were only three women at the townsite camp but the homes of the families are remembered by the single men as havens from the regular camp life. Most of the women were married but a number of single ladies arrived in Kitimat to fill office positions. These brave souls were out-numbered by one hundred to one and did not usually escape the camp without at least 20 proposals of marriage.

As people poured into the Kitimat Valley, many began to think of Kitimat as a place to settle. Alcan was promising modern homes at affordable rates, and a railway line to Terrace would soon link the isolated town to the rest of B.C. An overriding feeling of being part of a great pioneering adventure began to unfold, and Kitimat became a special place in the hearts of many.

Up until 1953, Kitimat had been the private undertaking of the Aluminum Company of Canada. Late in 1952, however, Alcan applied to the B.C. Legislature to have the 66 square miles of land at Kitimat incorporated as a district municipality. In the spring of the following year the Kitimat Incorporation Act was passed. Kitimat was no longer a company town. The people became the force behind the town's development and a Reeve and Council were elected.

To make an election possible, Alcan, who owned all the land, had to legally transfer land claims to candidates. Wilbur Sparks, an Alcan employee, became the town Reeve by acclamation and nine other men who had been made property owners, nominated each other for the six seats on Council. The 121 legal voters, (over 21 years old and six month's residence) elected: B.S. Baxter, E.G. Cronk, G. Davis, P.W. Hallman, G.T. Malby and Dr. Margetts to the first Council.

The municipality was born; under unique conditions. Never before had an unbuilt town without any permanent residents, been incorporated. The Municipality of Kitimat had no precedent, and as Reeve Sparks said: "Alcan wants Kitimat to be the perfect city. They are the people who will have to pay most of the taxes—we'd be foolish not to agree with them."

The Anderson Creek bridge in 1951. "Euchs and belly dumps were going 24 hours a day hauling gravel from the sandhill and I thought I'd never survive the noise …" Quote from Peter Bell, Alcan employee

The Hudson's Bay Company store at the Smeltersite Camp.

KITIMAT'S FIRST COUNCIL - 1953

Kitimat's First Council — 1953: From left to right: Municipal Engineer D.P.I. Hawkins; Councillors B.S. Baxter, E.G. Cronk, P.G. Margetts; Municipal Manager C. McC. Henderson; Reeve W.H. Sparks; Deputy Clerk Miss Y. Mearns; Councillors G.T. Malby, G.M.K. Davis, P.W. Hallman; Treasurer L.W. Wheeldon.
Photograph at first council from "Kitimat — The First Five Years", written by P. Meldrum.

The six lonely Councilmen, as they were once referred to, adopted a unique Code which provided for the hiring of a Municipal Manager to direct the administration of all the functions of the municipality. In July of '53 Cyril Henderson was appointed to that post. There were hundreds of things to be done, by-laws to be passed and proposals drafted before people could move into Kitimat proper. Aubrey Creed became Fire Chief and the first firefighting equipment was bought. A contract with the RCMP was signed, the School Board was elected and a bridge over the Kitimat River was completed, at a cost of over a million dollars. Sewers and water systems were planned and finally, the Nechako Neighbourhood, Kitimat's first residential area, was constructed.

Neighbourhood "A", Nechako under construction: August 13, 1954.

Houses floating in the Douglas Channel.
Many of the homes were pre-fabricated in the
south and barged to Kitimat, ca. 1955.

Men working on homes in the
Nechako neighbourhood. Johnson-
Crooks construction men "move from
house to house repetitively doing
the same few specialized jobs."

View looking down Kingfisher Avenue
from the present location of the B.C.
Telephone office, ca. 1954.

Staff photograph of the men and women who built Kitimat's first houses.

Kitimat in early 1954 was hardly recognizable as a town; from the smelter and camp one could have driven along the rough road and over the Anderson Creek Bridge. Then came the sandhill in the distance, considerably shrunken, but still only yards from the riverbank. The Service Centre was a field of stumps, bulldozers and fires, and just over the Kitimat bridge lay the townsite camp. Around a few more curves, along the rough road and up a recently graded hill was the residential area—some of the houses complete, others just foundations—and everywhere, bulldozers overturned earth and mud. One might expect it to look rough, but after only three years of construction, it was a wonder how far things had progressed.

At the end of 1954, Kitimat was a substantially different place. In that year production began at the smelter, the Nechako Centre was completed, and the first houses occupied. Prince Philip, the Duke of Edinburgh, was the guest of honour at the official opening ceremony at the smelter.

Whitaker wrote humorously of the making of Kitimat's first ingot: "In no time the metal flowed out and I had His Highness start the casting and cooling machine—again cameras flashed. We then congregated around the discharge end of the casting machine to await the first ingot. Mr. Powell then presented a miniature souvenir ingot saying, 'Your Highness, here is a replica of the first ingot cast at Kitimat. We would like you to have it.' The Duke taking it, looked at it, then at the first ingot and said, 'Replica? You call this a replica!—that (pointing to the large ingot) says, Alcan—this says Kitimat.' The next day one of the Vancouver newspapers came out with a large headline: 'Alcan tries to spoof the Duke'."

That first ingot signaled production for the first two potlines at Kitimat. There was to be further lines constructed and eventually Alcan would employ almost 3,000 workers.

Chapter VI
Settling In

Production at the aluminum smelter signaled the beginning of the end of Kitimat's heady years of construction. In June of 1954, a month prior to the smelter's official August opening, the Johnson-Crooks Construction Company who had undertaken a housing program in Neighbourhood A, or Nechako, expressed confidence that their first units would be ready for occupation by September 1st. Their long-range plan called for a total of 300 homes to be completed by December 1st, 1954.

Mr. Copeland, the Project Manager for the American-based company, told a Northern Sentinel reporter the secrets for getting work done rapidly in isolated conditions. "We prefabricate nothing but build right on the site. However, we try to operate on an adaptation of the assembly-line principle. Men move from house to house repetitively doing the same few specialized jobs." The Johnson-Crooks houses were to be one-and-a-half storey duplexes. At this time the Hullah Construction Company had already completed 38 houses and in mid-June, 32 of these were already occupied. These houses were different from those planned by the Johnson-Crooks Company. They had been prefabricated in the south and barged up to Kitimat, and had the luxury of fireplaces in the living rooms. The local paper reported that the tenants were satisfied with their new houses on the hill.

Alcan had evolved a highly unique mortgage plan for its employees at Kitimat. It meant that Alcan's employees could buy a new house in the townsite with a down payment as low as five percent. The Central Housing and Mortgage Company, along with Alcan had arranged to finance the first mortgages on houses meeting their specifications. Alcan further assisted its permanent employees by offering a second mortgage. If the purchaser faithfully paid his taxes, and kept up with payments, Alcan would give him a monthly bonus that could be applied to the cost of the house. It was a wonderful scheme that allowed many young families the chance to buy a home, something that in other towns would have been an impossible dream.

In September of '54 there was a public auction of 118 building lots in that first neighbourhood. This was also part of Alcan's long-term plan and was in line with the Company's policy to make a quarter of all the building lots available for private sale. Prices for the lots ranged from $880.00 to $1,050.00. The catch was that a permanent house had to be built within 18 months of the purchase of the property.

By December, hundreds of new homes were completed at the townsite, and families were pouring into Kitimat. Elva Craig, wife of Clare Craig, a foreman at Alcan, arrived in December when their house on Heron Street was ready. Many other people arrived about the same time, and Mr. Craig recalled, "that all the furniture was down at the dock in pallet boards with tarps over them. What a horrible mess—we couldn't find our fridge for a week."

Pat Wiens, wife of Art Wiens, was another of the December '54 arrivals. Art recalled his impressions of life at the new townsite in an Ingot article of 1974. "The first morning, I took my bright new shining aluminum lunch bucket and put it under my arm, my wife saw me to the door, I kissed her, and then looked down Quail Street and all along the street this thing was being repeated—everyone had an identical house, an identical lunch bucket and I'll swear an identical wife!" That was life in the modern aluminum city!

There were people from all walks of life from many countries and all of them adapting to a new way of life in the brand new town of Kitimat. "It was an exciting experience", recalled June Hannah. "You would ask how long someone had been here and they would say 'two weeks'."

Many of those newcomers remembered those early days with fondness. There was a feeling of belonging to a great adventure out of which grew a strong community spirit. Stan Rough, a well-known Kitimatian, wrote that "the newness of Kitimat was the greatest challenge." He continued, "There is a good blending here of prairie people, native sons, back easterners, British Islers, Europeans and even some from the South Pacific. They all have one thing in common; they are friendly and have pulled up stakes back home to build a new city. The people here are building their own organizations and traditions will grow.

Kitimat in the mid-fifties was strikingly different than it is now. The roads weren't paved and there was a daily battle with mud. Children played in it and vehicles got stuck in it. There was no need for licensing cars either, because one couldn't drive anywhere except in Kitimat between the townsite and smeltersite. It wasn't until 1957 that a road to Terrace was completed, at which time many cars were sent by barge from Vancouver and later by train.

The Nechako Centre opened in 1954. It was the townsite's first shopping mall. The supermarket was opened in the fall and made grocery shopping much easier for the growing population. The Sheardown store had a coffee bar that became a popular spot for the townsite's shoppers. Art and Olie Coghlin opened Coghlin Hardware in December 1954 in a small space near the grocery store. It was also a men's clothing store and a Simpson Sears order office. Until 1955, and the completion of the Nechako Elementary School, classes were held in a large commercial space at Nechako Centre. The older children were bused to the smeltersite where there was a small school. Later on, Coghlin Hardware took over that same space at the Centre and expanded to become Kitimat's largest hardware store. In those early days Nechako Centre was a bustle of activity; there was a post office where residents could pick up mail, doctors moved into the offices above the shops and later the Nechako Theatre and the Kitimat Public Library opened. All of this further added to the Centre's community flavour.

The next important step forward for Kitimat came with the building of a rail link between Terrace and Kitimat. The completion of this line meant that Kitimat was, for the first time, connected by efficient overland transportation to all of North America. Albert Whitaker had spent months negotiating with the Canadian National Railroad for a line to Kitimat. He wrote, "It became my responsibility to get Canadian National to build a branch line from Terrace to Kitimat. So at the earliest date—it must have been in early 1951—we began negotiating."

The negotiations dragged out for months. In the meantime the CN engineers were surveying the route and estimating its cost. One of the stumbling blocks to agreement was the Canadian National's insistence on our (Alcan's) guarantee of an average of a million dollars revenue per year for ten years. The President of the CNR claimed that he had to have such a guarantee "to prevent every Tom, Dick or Harry insisting on free branch lines into their plants."

Nechako Centre opened in the fall of 1954.
Here it is surrounded by the ever-present
mud following the grand opening.

Crossing the Kitimat River in 1954 before the bridge was built.

Eventually an agreement was signed and ratified by the Canadian Parliament. However, Whitaker recalls that the members of Parliament gave the Alcan negotiators a hard time. He wrote, "Finally I was called on to explain why we needed the branch line, etc., and at the end of my explanation a very prominent member said, 'Mr. Whitaker, are you satisfied with the deal that you got from the CN?' to which I replied, 'Your Honour, I'm glad you asked that question. The answer is we are not, for it seems to us that Alcan, a privately-owned company that has the courage to go into the wilderness of British Columbia and commit itself to an undertaking of the order of five hundred million dollars, should not have to make a guarantee. Surely the Government should take that much risk on this new development considering what we are taking." Whitaker managed to get a round of applause for his honesty but no change in the contract.

The people at Kitimat applauded too when the first scheduled train came into Kitimat, January 17, 1955. There were over 100 people aboard and rumours had it that numerous cases of rum accompanied them. The return trip left Kitimat with 50 celebrants aboard and hauling five carloads of ingots. An article in The Province remarked that the train was actually "fifty years behind schedule," thus harking back to the railway dreams of the Grand Trunk Pacific days. When the last spike was set in place on July 8, 1955 and the train station officially opened, the occasion was celebrated with speeches, banners and great splendour. Hundreds of people came out on that day for the official opening up of Kitimat to the rest of the world.

In the years to follow, many Kitimatians would utilize the CN service to Terrace. It became a usual practice for shoppers to take the train to Terrace for the day that is until Highway 25 was completed in 1957. The growing community could not hold or attract new settlers without that road link. It was still too isolated.

In 1954, an editorial in the local paper expressed anger at the Provincial Government's lack of interest in the Terrace-Kitimat road link. It seems that survey work had been completed by 1954 but the Honourable P. A. Gaglardi, the Highway Minister at the time, felt that "there was no loose money" available to begin construction. This statement seemed frivolous in the light that the Provincial Government stood to collect many dollars in taxes resulting from the Alcan development.

Celebrations on July 8, 1955 for the driving of the last spike on the Terrace/ Kitimat rail link. Photo by David S. Boyer © 1956 National Geographic Society.

When the road construction finally did begin in 1955, it was beset with difficulties. Weather didn't always cooperate and there were a number of bridges to be built and tons of earth to be blasted away before the road's final completion in November of 1957. P. Gaglardi was under constant pressure to keep up a fast pace on the road construction. When the road was finally opened, Gaglardi was present to snip the ribbon and commented, "I don't know any people in B.C. who can give me orders in such short time than the people of Kitimat and Terrace."

The road to Terrace truly brought Kitimat closer to the rest of the world. The two communities, separated by 36 miles, were proclaimed sisters. Going to Terrace for an evening out became a popular activity, and on Saturday mornings the road to Terrace was always busy with shoppers. The road connection also opened up camping areas at Lakelse significantly, adding to Kitimat's recreation possibilities.

With a road out and a rail link, Kitimat had become a growing concern. Neighbourhood C, or Kildala, was slowly being built up. Construction on the modern Kitimat General Hospital was begun, and the City Centre shopping mall was officially opened in 1956. The Northern Sentinel reported that "Hundreds of early morning shoppers witnessed the opening of the new Hudson's Bay Company and Super Valu stores. A light snow flurry added a sparkle to the festive atmosphere as eager pre-Christmas shoppers waited to see their new stores. Mrs. Radley, wife of the Aluminum

Company's B.C. Project Manager personally welcomed the lady shoppers and presented each with an orchid, a gift from the Hudson's Bay Company."

Kitimat residents were always celebrating something in those first ten years. Trade licenses were being issued constantly as businessmen took advantage of the prospering town. David Chow who had opened Helen's Cafe at Anderson Creek camp in 1955, moved into a $100,000 ultra-modern cafe at the City Centre in 1957. It had been a popular spot at its old location and continued to serve the Kitimat public until 1970. One of the outstanding features, remembered well by Helen's clientele, was the large mural in the dining room. It depicted various stages of the aluminum industry in Kitimat and Kemano.

Another early business at Kitimat was Lakelse Valley Milk Products operated by George Thom and his father, Jim. George Thom related to Kerryl Mix how it was that his family had ventured into the north. "We came to Kitimat for five years to make our fortune. We never quite made it so we are still here." A modest statement from a very successful man who became mayor of Kitimat, raised a family of four children, and maintained strong business interests in the town.

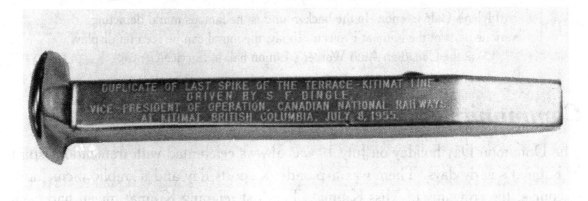

Souvenir aluminum spike struck in Montreal and engraved at Birks, Vancouver, to commemorate the completion of the Terrace-Kitimat link.

Helen's Café interior. In the background is the famous mural depicting
various parts of the Kitimat Project. Today, the mural can be seen on display
at the Canadian Auto Worker's Union hall in Service Centre.

Community Celebration

The Dominion Day holiday on July 1ˢᵗ was always celebrated with tremendous spirit
in Kitimat's early days. There was a parade, a sports day and a public picnic and,
of course, the crowning of Miss Kitimat. The first reigning Kitimat queen had been
Terry Coghlin in 1954. In 1957, Annette Heraka was crowned Miss Kitimat. She
was interviewed following the ceremony and remarked on the 4,000-strong bachelor
population, calling them wolves—but nice wolves! There were still plenty of single men
in Kitimat; in fact, they almost constituted half of Kitimat's population of 10,000.

Alcan's Recreation Director and the Recreation Director hired by the Municipality
were given the job of diverting the excess energies of the population. There was an art
group, a Little Symphony, and a well-attended program of night school classes—
English for new Canadians being one of the most popular and essential classes. By
1958, there were also 11 soccer teams in Kitimat.

Soccer games were a popular spectator sport. There were reportedly over 300 avid
soccer fans at the Sunday games which were held at the smeltersite field. It seems the
soccer crowds were a passionate lot, as is evidenced by a headline in The Northern
Sentinel from August of 1956: "Sunday Soccer Ends in a Riot". The article begins,

"A riot involving spectators and soccer players in the Portuguese community of Kitimat and the Riverside United teams, Sunday evening has resulted in the Portuguese team being completely disqualified from future play. Security guards were called to quiet the disturbance. Referee George Madden was injured." The Haisla of Kitamaat also took part in the league, and all in all, the game served to bring the diverse ethnic groups of Kitimat closer together.

"Miss Kitimat 1954" Terry Voitchovski (née Coghlin) and "Miss Kitimat 1977" Carrie Paul, at Riverlodge, March 31, 1978.

There was an art group, Little Symphony, and well attended programs of night school courses.

Fishing boats from Kitamaat Village served as ferries for Kitimatians eager to watch the Haisla team play soccer against the teams from Kitimat. There was no road linking the two communities and schoolchildren and smelter workers had to make a boat trip daily from the Village, ca. 1957.

One of the many floats that took part in the 1958 Dominion Day parade. In the background is the logged-off and bare Haisla Hill

Kitimat Growing Up

An article on Kitimat in Macleans Magazine, published in 1958, noted that there was hardly any old people and "there is a single girl to every ten bachelors." That article, written by Pierre Burton, commented: "There is little overt trouble, only a vague sense of isolation and in some quarters a certain dissatisfaction with the community's disciplined perfection." Kitimat was a strange mix of bachelors and families. In 1958, there were 3,500 children and in a population of 9,000 it was a significant number. In fact, Kitimat was in the throes of a baby boom and was referred to by the residents as the "pregnant valley." It was also humorously noted that of the 120 women living in Kitimat in 1956, 150 of them were expecting. Despite the highly publicized birth control pill development in 1957, children continued to be born at the rate of approximately 300 per year. Families who had considered Kitimat a place to make a fast dollar were changing their minds and settling into the new life.

It was a surprise that Kitimat had become the kind of town Alcan had hoped for. It was now a place where people took initiative, made themselves feel at home, and stayed put to raise families.

Many of the people who came to Kitimat in the fifties heard of the town in magazines or were directed to Alcan by advertisements in newspapers across the country. Len Hurl came to Kitimat after reading an article about the new wilderness community. The Reader's Digest gave the new town of Kitimat space on its pages as well.

For its 40th anniversary, Alcan published a tribute to its employees who came to Kitimat in 1956. The pamphlet related the circumstances that brought men and families to Kitimat. Many of the Alcan old timers recalled the opportunities offered by Alcan because of the steady work. Others remembered with a chuckle their first impressions of the town. Walter Pavlakovich recalled "that his first look at Kitimat was not encouraging. There was snow and mud right up to your . . . But," he says "if I had it to do all over again I would do it the same way. Kitimat has been good to me and my family." Hans Diesing, another '56 arrival remembers his first day at Kitimat as "a dull day. But then again between the train station and the motel there wasn't a lot to see." He hadn't intended staying for 25 years but like many of his fellow employees, Hans and his wife Dorothea raised a family in Kitimat.

Joe Vales arrived in Kitimat five weeks after leaving Portugal. He recalls, "Everything was different. I wasn't used to the weather before I came here. I hadn't ever seen snow before." Joe Feldhoff explained in the tribute, "Money meant a lot to us newcomers. So when I heard of the high wages they were paying, a $1.67 an hour at that time, I decided to come to Kitimat."

Although the cash dividends of living in Kitimat attracted employees, the wilderness recreation possibilities held many of them to the area. Erwin Miserre typifies that interest. "Kitimat was a paradise when I arrived. I bought a boat right away. I love waterskiing or just exploring in a boat." Other Kitimatians enjoyed fishing, hunting and hiking in the area.

There is an interesting story about one of the first hikes to the summit of Mount Elizabeth. It seems that the group who travelled from the smeltersite to the base and then up to the majestic mountain, decided to christen the peak after one of the women at the smeltersite — Elizabeth. Of course it was the year of Queen Elizabeth's coronation so the name seemed especially apt. Surprisingly the mountain had been similarly christened in the earlier pioneering days by a Government surveyor called Monckton. He had graciously named the snow-capped peak after Elizabeth Anderson. So it seems the mountain was destined to bear the name it has today.

It is apparent when reading of or speaking to the early residents of Kitimat that life was good in the early days. Everyone knew almost everybody else and people seemed to get along. The isolation and the residents' commonalities—all having left friends and home behind and nearly all working at the smelter—made for a strong sense of community.

Not everyone who came to Kitimat in the 1950's had been assured a job. Some had to wait a number of weeks or return at a later date to get a position at the smelter. However, before 1957 there was little unemployment. Kitimat, in fact was rated as one of the wealthiest communities for its size in Canada. In 1957, it was worth four times the assessed value of Prince Rupert and Prince George. However, in the late 1950's the aluminum market dropped bringing a slump at Kitimat. In 1957, the Aluminum Company of Canada shelved plans to expand the smelter. That postponement brought about the largest concentrated layoff in Kitimat's short history. Five potlines were in operation at the time but construction of lines 7 and 8 was halted. Merchants were also worried at that time, fearing that the layoffs would dangerously limit local commerce.

An English class for new Canadians, October 2, 1957. From left to right: Frieda Meuser (Germany); Jacob Hadland (Norway); Frank Gunur (Austria), and Christa Mais (Portugal).

Lineups were long at the unemployment office. Mr. Musgrove, head of the office, reported, "Every morning the office is literally crammed to the doors with men looking for work. Men are standing shoulder to shoulder." Some of the unemployed construction crews found work clearing snow and others tried to get permanent positions with the Aluminum Company of Canada at the smelter.

The permanent employees at the smelter seemed secure in spite of the many layoffs of construction workers, but in 1961 the entire operation was shut down to make repairs to the Kemano Tunnel. One thousand three hundred workers were laid off for almost three months. One reporter who visited the town following the layoffs in '61 wrote, "There were dozens of empty construction barracks and temporary buildings. There were boarded-up houses and a stockpile of construction parts at the smeltersite." The effect of the layoffs was not permanent, and in September of 1961 all of the 1,300 workers were rehired.

The changes in the aluminum market did have an effect on the Aluminum Company of Canada and the residents' attitude at Kitimat. The plans for the town were scaled down and at that time Geoff Whitehead, Alcan's Property Manager told Allan Fotheringham of the Vancouver Sun, "Alcan was never thinking in terms of 50,000 people. That was merely the economic unit that planners quoted in their scheme. For the residents the ups and downs of the aluminum market served to illustrate the need for further industry at Kitimat."

In the early 1960's it was rumoured that Kitimat would be the site for a pulp mill development. The one-industry town had been actively campaigning for development and Kitimat seemed a logical site for a pulp mill.

However the mill site was not to be at Kitimat, Prince George was chosen instead. Yet it was only six years later that Eurocan Pulp and Paper Company Limited decided that Kitimat offered the best location for their planned expansion. When completed the Eurocan pulp mill and logging operations employed approximately 1,200 workers. It was a great addition to Kitimat and served to further the dreams for an industrial centre in the valley.

In 1981 a methanol plant was opened in Kitimat. These new industries meant the end of Kitimat as a one industry town and the beginning of a new phase. This phase would be different from the earlier, wilder days of the 1950's but in some ways closer to the planner's vision of a northern centre with a strong economic base and continued cultural development.

Conclusion

Kitimat today is the sum of its rich past. Its heritage is one of diversity and abrupt change. Each of its three phases may be traced back to that brave man Hunclee-qualas who first entered this valley and invited people of all nations to come join him. It was he who started Kitimat's first industry, the eulachon harvest, and set the tone of Kitimat as a production centre with wide-ranging trade connections.

The first pioneer settlers to this valley were not misfits escaping a too modern world but men and women with vision who were willing to live in isolation and through hardship in the belief that their northern home would one day be a bustling centre of commerce and culture. Kitimat was then, for a time, bypassed by the railway and routes by sea leaving the early pioneers isolated and unable to sell their produce.

But Hunclee-qualas's people survived and once again a wave of newcomers came to Kitimat to build a new town. Many of these new pioneers still live in Kitimat today and remind us that from the drama of history springs hopes for tomorrow.

James Tirrul-Jones (Museum Curator, 1981-1987)

A Short Bibliography

A Tribute to 25 Years 1956-1981, 1981. Kitimat: Alcan Smelters and Chemicals Ltd.

Casey Sez. 1951-53. Kitimat: Kitimat Constructors.

Horetzky, C., 1880, Some Startling Facts Relating to the Canadian Pacific Railway and the Northwest Lands. Ottawa: Free Press.

The Ingot, 1954- , Kitimat: Aluminum Company of Canada.

"Kitimat: A New City" in Architectural Forum, July 1954.

Lopatin, Ivan A., 1945. Social Life and Religion of the Indians in Kitimat, British Columbia. Los Angeles: University of Calif. Press.

McFadden, Isobel, 1971, Living by Bells.

Meldrum, Hugh, Honestly it Happened. Unpublished Ms.: Kitimat Centennial Museum Archives.

Meldrum, Pixie, 1958, Kitimat: The First Five Years. Kitimat: The Corporation of the District of Kitimat.

Nichol, Julie, Ed., The Voices of Kitimat 1967. Kitimat: Northern Sentinel Press.

The Northern Sentinel, 1954-1982. Kitimat: Northern Sentinel Press.

Olson, R.L., 1940, "The Social Organization of the Haisla of British Columbia" in Anthropological Records, Vol. 2. No 5. Berkeley: University of Calif. Press.

Pritchard, John C., 1977. Economic Development and the Disintegration of Traditional Culture Among the Haisla. University of British Columbia: Unpublished Thesis.

Raley, G.H., Ed., 1893-1906, Na-Na-Kwa. Kitimat: Rv. G.H. Raley.

Robinson, Gordon, 1956, Tales of Kitamaat. Kitimat: Northern Sentinel Press.

Rogerson, Rita, 1953, "Reminiscences of Kitimat - Before 'ALCAN'" in Northern Digest March, 1953.

Rough, Stan et. al., 1955-1956, "Time and Place" in The Northern Sentinel. Kitimat: Northern Sentinel Press.

Varley, Elizabeth Anderson, 1981, Kitimat My Valley. Terrace: Northern Times Press.